The RESULTS TREE

The RESULTS TREE

A Proven Path to the
LIFE YOU *Really* WANT

GABRIEL GRIESS
FOUNDER, NAVIGATING LEADERS

The Results Tree
Copyright © 2026 by Gabriel Griess. All rights reserved.

Published by Harp & Sword Media LLC
129 S. Main St., #260
Grapevine, TX 76051
www.harpandswordmedia.com

Cover design by Bill Johnson

Unless otherwise noted, all Scripture quotations are taken from the Holy Bible, New International Version®, NIV®. Copyright © 1973, 1978, 1984, 2011 by Biblica, Inc.® Used by permission of Zondervan. All rights reserved worldwide. www.zondervan.com. The "NIV" and "New International Version" are trademarks registered in the United States Patent and Trademark Office by Biblica, Inc.®

Scripture quotations marked ESV are from The ESV® Bible (The Holy Bible, English Standard Version®), copyright © 2001 by Crossway, a publishing ministry of Good News Publishers. Used by permission. All rights reserved.

Scripture quotations marked NASB are taken from the (NASB®) New American Standard Bible®, Copyright © 1960, 1971, 1977, 1995, 2020 by The Lockman Foundation. Used by permission. All rights reserved. www.lockman.org

Scripture quotations marked NLT are taken from the *Holy Bible*, New Living Translation, copyright ©1996, 2004, 2015 by Tyndale House Foundation. Used by permission of Tyndale House Publishers, Carol Stream, Illinois 60188. All rights reserved.

Names in this book are real, modified, or fictional, depending on permissions and individual desires.

While the publisher has made every effort to provide accurate internet addresses at the time of publication, neither the publisher nor the author assumes any responsibility for errors or for changes that occur after publication. Further, the publisher does not have any control over and does not assume any responsibility for author or third-party websites or their content.

ISBN (jacketed hardcover): 979-8-99150-807-0
ISBN (ebook): 979-8-99150-803-2

10 9 8 7 6 5 4 3 2 1

Printed in the United States of America

*To my family—Kristie, Preston, Mikayla "MG," and Harrison—
your love is my anchor, and your belief in me is my fuel.*

*Thank you for walking this journey with me, for your patience
during the long hours, for the laughter that lifted hard days, and
for being the inspiration behind my pursuit of purpose.*

*This book is a reflection of the life we are building together, rooted in
faith, driven by vision, and sustained by the love of God and one another.*

*With all my heart,
Gabriel (Daddy)*

Contents

Foreword by Keith Bentz.. ix
Introduction.. xiii

Chapter 1 From a Different Angle.. 1
Chapter 2 Vision: The Necessary Roots............................ 25
Chapter 3 Connecting Goals to Your Vision....................... 59
Chapter 4 Clear Intentions: Goals That Really Matter......... 101
Chapter 5 Committed Action: Choose—Now!..................... 123
Chapter 6 Results: The Life You Really Want.................... 155
Chapter 7 Enjoy the Journey!.. 173

Appendix A Uncovering Your Life's Vision....................... 195
Appendix B SMART Goals 207
Appendix C Becoming Self-Aware: A Guided Self-Discovery Exercise 213
Appendix D Ten Traits You Can Cultivate 223

Continue Your Journey 225
How Salvation Works: A Simple Invitation...................... 227
Acknowledgments 229
Endnotes... 231

Foreword

It's not about if you fail, but when. People who are attempting great things invariably experience big setbacks. It's part of the territory. It may be a bit trite, but it's true: The road to success is paved with lessons learned through failure.
Gabriel Griess

When Gabriel Griess asked me to write a foreword to *The Results Tree*, I was honored because Gabriel Griess is a man I deeply admire and respect. As you'll discover in the pages ahead, Gabriel's purpose in writing this book is the same as his purpose for everything he does in his life: genuinely to contribute. It's not to build his reputation, not to make money, but to make a positive difference in as many people's lives as possible. That's what Gabriel does in every aspect of his life, which is why his writing rings true and will inspire you.

What you have in store in the following pages is not some armchair academician's theories about leadership or some motivational speaker's polished clichés about how to achieve success. What you have is the story of Gabriel's own personal journey of overcoming self-doubt and self-sabotage, breaking through limiting beliefs, and discovering for himself how to live a life worth living.

Gabriel is a hands-on, down-to-earth, salt-of-the-earth kind of guy who learned to succeed from his own failures and by honestly confronting his own shortcomings as a man, a husband, a father, and a leader in his company. His life is a perfect illustration of what the book is all about: the power of an inspiring vision, the courage to never give up in the face of setbacks, and the resilience to bounce back and learn from his mistakes, even after sabotaging himself. It's a story I'm sure you can relate to because Gabriel owes his success not to some special gift or talent, or to having a genius-level IQ, but to his unwavering commitment to living a life worth living and leaving behind a memorable legacy. And that commitment, and the success it brings with it, is a choice that's available to each one of us.

Many books about optimal performance are filled with theories and advice that leave you with good ideas but not much to support you in putting into action new behaviors and new ways of looking at the world. *The Results Tree* provides you with a proven structure and specific daily practices to move step-by-step toward success. Over the course of the book, you'll have the opportunity to discover an authentic vision and purpose for your life that will energize and motivate you. You'll be guided to set specific and measurable goals to support yourself in turning your vision into reality. You'll clarify for yourself the specific actions you'll need to take to turn your goals into solid achievements. You'll understand the importance of having people in your life whom you can count on to support and challenge you and give you honest feedback. And you'll be inspired by Gabriel's stories of how he used his mistakes, his failures, and the times he sabotaged himself as valuable lessons rather than reasons for giving up.

But more important than a method for achieving results, *The Results Tree* is a book about how to live your life from moment to moment so that you experience joy and fulfillment, whatever your level of success in the external world. The key to this, for Gabriel, is to come from being in service, to approach every situation in life from the mindset "What can I contribute? How can I make a positive difference?" With examples from his work, his marriage, his parenting, and his relationship with his father, Gabriel shows us the power of being in service to create the deeply fulfilling experience of life that all of us are searching for.

I've come to believe I serve people best by sharing what I've learned from my own missteps. My failures have become tools. When I help others grow, I grow too. That's how I pay it forward.
GABRIEL GRIESS

As you'll discover in the following pages, Gabriel is personally a devout Christian. His unshakable faith in God and in Christ as his Savior gives him tremendous certainty and a calm inner strength. At the same time, because he feels loved and accepted by God for who he really is (both the good news and the bad news), he is able to be fully open and honest about the mistakes he's made, the times he's let himself and others down, without having to hide his faults behind a facade of superiority. This willingness to reveal himself frees Gabriel to share openly how he turned failures, breakdowns, and even self-sabotage into valuable learning opportunities, and how clear intention and committed action can overcome the setbacks that are inevitable whenever we declare risky, challenging goals.

And even though he trusts in God to guide his actions, Gabriel holds himself fully responsible for the choices he makes and for the consequences of his choices and actions. He lives and breathes the responsible person's motto: "If it's to be, it's up to me." This means giving up being a victim of circumstances, giving up blaming others and yourself, and taking 100 percent responsibility for your experience of events as they come along.

The sincerity of Gabriel's belief in God and in Christ as his Savior comes through loud and clear in the pages of this book. I am not a Christian, but for me Gabriel's religious beliefs did not detract from or in any way contradict what he has to say about vision, clear intention, responsibility, and committed action. At no time in reading *The Results Tree* did I feel criticized or made wrong for not sharing Gabriel's beliefs.

So welcome to *The Results Tree*. To create maximum value for yourself in reading this book, be sure to take the time to do the exercises at the end of each chapter. They are designed to support you in putting the concepts and insights in the book into daily practices that can change your life.

Enjoy!

Keith Bentz

Master Trainer

Introduction

It is not enough to have a vision. In order to have its power, you must enact your vision on earth for all to see. Only then do you have the power.
Nicholas "Black Elk"

All of us have areas in our lives we've avoided—issues we haven't confronted, habits we haven't broken, conversations we haven't had, commitments we have failed to keep to others and, more importantly, to ourselves. We push these things aside, hoping they'll fix themselves, or that we'll get to them eventually. If we're honest, we know the truth: These areas are out of alignment with the kind of life we say we really want. When we ignore what's broken or out of place, we set the stage to sabotage our own success.

As you begin the journey of The Results Tree, it's critical to understand this: Lasting results don't take root in faulty soil. Failing to address the parts of your life that are misaligned—relationships, behaviors, addictions, resentments—doesn't just slow your progress. It sets you up to fail. I've done it. More than once. In this book I share five personal stories of how I blew up my own progress by refusing to take responsibility. Think of those ignored areas like live grenades. You can make a lot of progress outwardly, but eventually, one of them detonates, and all that good work gets leveled.

The truth is, misalignment doesn't just delay your growth; it erodes your energy, weakens your relationships, and slowly chips away at your confidence and integrity. Ignoring it is not neutral. It's expensive and has consequences. You're not the only one who pays the price when you live out of alignment. Think of the people you care about whose lives are impacted when you're out of integrity with yourself.

This isn't an *either-or* proposition. It's *both* and *and*. The time to start the journey toward your vision and take yourself on is now. You don't need to wait until your life is perfect to begin. But you do need to commit to making cleaning up what's out of alignment the first step in your growth plan. Remember, you didn't get off course overnight and you won't get back on course in a single weekend. Step by step, day by day, you can align your actions with your intentions, creating new habits that support you in achieving your purpose.

As Lao Tzu wrote twenty-five hundred years ago in the *Tao Te Ching*, "A journey of a thousand miles begins with a single step." Are you ready to take that step?

Inside you is a clearer, wiser, more grounded version of yourself, and that person is worth fighting for. Only you can do the fighting. You will feel resistance, maybe even physical or emotional discomfort. That's not a sign something's wrong. That's proof that something is finally shifting. This is how your transformation begins, by owning your vision, taking radical responsibility, serving something greater than yourself, and choosing courageous action again and again.

Before you move to the next page, I challenge you to name one area of your life that's out of alignment. Write it down. Circle it. Don't judge yourself for it. Just commit to facing it head-on. You are not a finished product. You are becoming. Let this be the moment you stop drifting and start building. Go to what's hard, what you have been avoiding, and know that the shortest distance to your destination is through the center of what you've been avoiding.

Note: This is your book. The lines give you room to write, so grab a pen and dive in. The goal isn't to fill in the blanks but to think deeply and imagine what your life can become. This is the first step in crystallizing your vision.

| Watch for QR codes like this throughout the book that connect you to resources including downloads, worksheets, and guided exercises designed to help you put these principles into practice.

Let me give you some guidelines for using the book and exercises. Read each chapter. In fact, I encourage you to read it three times. The first time, you'll start to be familiar with the concepts; the second time, you'll find deeper meaning; and the third time, you'll really get it and be able to apply the principles presented. Then, work through the associated exercises. This isn't a timed drill. You don't get extra points for finishing before anyone else. So take your time, think, ask yourself hard questions, and wrestle with the answers. Patience and persistence will pay off, I promise.

In the chapters underline points that stand out to you, and in the exercises go beyond the questions and prompts. You may feel compelled to call someone to talk about what you're learning, write an email or two, or research a point more thoroughly. Consider this book your personal journal. Write, reflect, write some more, and return to these pages from time to time to reinforce the principles.

Use this book as if your life depends on it. My prayer is that in time the pages are creased from too many reads, corners are dog-eared, and passages are highlighted and underlined, with the cover barely hanging on.

I hope this book makes you uncomfortable. I want to challenge your previous assumptions about how life works, expose excuses for remaining stuck in self-limiting habits, and inspire you to reach further and higher than ever. If you notice internal pushback or a trigger as you read, that's by design.

I'll share a thought that has kept me going, which may be helpful to you.

Remember those *Choose Your Own Adventure* books you may have read as a kid? You'd turn the page, read the story, and suddenly be faced with a choice: If you open the mysterious door, turn to page 42. If you run down the hallway, turn to page 88. With every decision the story shifted, sometimes toward triumph, sometimes toward peril, but always forward. Life, it turns out, is a lot like that.

Because of our free will, we are living a *Choose Your Own Adventure* story, only this one was written by the Author of the universe. God crafted the narrative with divine love, purpose, and possibility. He left the choices to you. Every decision becomes a page turned. Every moment is a fork in the road.

God wants you to be the hero of your own journey, not just a passenger or a passive reader, but a bold, curious, courageous participant. Stay close to Him—consult the Author often—and the rest will take care of itself.

Let the adventure begin!

Chapter 1

FROM A DIFFERENT ANGLE

*Always dream and shoot higher than you know you can do.
Do not bother just to be better than your contemporaries
or predecessors. Try to be better than yourself.*
WILLIAM FAULKNER

I was seventeen, sitting alone in our dusty Nebraska farmhouse, the hum of the tractors outside barely masking the storm inside my chest. I held the Air Force Academy admissions catalog in my hands, creased from too many reads, corners dog-eared, the cover barely hanging on. I had stared at the photos so many times I could describe the chapel's jagged spires in my sleep. Flying jets. Becoming an officer. Leaving the fields behind and stepping into a world I had only seen in movies and magazines. It wasn't just a dream; it was *the* dream.

There was only one problem: Almost everything around me said it was impossible.

2 The Results Tree

We didn't know anyone who had gone to a service academy. We weren't from the right town and only loosely associated with the right power brokers. I wasn't the smartest, strongest, or most acclaimed candidate, but something inside me refused to let go. That vision had taken root, and no matter how unlikely it seemed, I couldn't shake it. Every morning before school I worked out alone in the dark. I studied harder than anyone I knew. I wrote and rewrote my essays, hunted down recommendation letters, and tracked my congressman's staff to secure a nomination. I still remember the look on my guidance counselor's face when I told him where I was applying. He didn't say it, but his eyes did: "Good luck, kid. Don't get your hopes up."

I kept going, not because I was fearless but because the vision was louder than the fear.

That pursuit became my first real lesson in what I call The Results Tree: vision, clear intention, and committed action. At seventeen I didn't have a name for it. I just knew that I wasn't going to give up. Even when I was rejected the first time. Even when I had to rearrange everything to make it happen. Even when the path was longer, messier, and lonelier than I ever expected. I'll share more of that story later, but here's what I want you to know before we go any further: You don't need perfection. You don't need to have it all figured out. You just need a vision that calls you forward, a plan grounded in intention, and the guts to keep going when it gets hard.

That's what The Results Tree is all about.

The concept of this book has enormous power in its simplicity, and the process yields the results you've always dreamed of. The Results Tree is a distillation of years of research and contemplation and, to be honest, plenty of trial and error. Effective and predictable results are the product of being grounded in your vision and purpose. Then, clear intention directs and motivates committed action. This has worked for thousands of people, and it will work for you. It doesn't matter where you find yourself right now. You can use this concept whether you're wildly successful or you're lost in a loop and not sure where to take your next step.

So what's the problem? Why is it so hard to achieve goals that matter? It's easy to drift away from sound principles and effective practices. Our planning, goal setting, and execution can fail at any point in the process, and for very different reasons. If we examine these failures, we can identify four types of people: paralyzed, plagued, preoccupied, and purposeful.

1. Paralyzed—Some people feel stuck, trapped by fear, doubt, or low expectations, sometimes by their own low expectations for themselves and sometimes by the low expectations of people around them. They want change but can't seem to move forward. The vision is foggy, the steps feel overwhelming, and so they stay right where they are, hoping something will shift on its own.

    Little children are naturally inquisitive and creative, constantly in the process of discovery, failure, and learning, which naturally produces positive results. When they feel affirmed in their innovative pursuits, creativity becomes second nature to them. Some people have suffered hard knocks, hard enough and long enough to crush the inherent spark that's inside them. They've become resigned to their lot in life. Nothing really excites them, and they avoid people and situations that challenge them. They live with the nagging sense of being "less than," and this self-perception has become completely normal.

2. Plagued—Some people are confused and discouraged by the way their lives have gone.

   These people are desperate, overwhelmed, and distressed, and they're willing to try anything to turn things around. They're searching for answers outside of themselves. They hope the next podcast, the next seminar, the next fitness program, the next diet, the next house, or the next spouse will be the spark that ignites the chain reaction of change that will make their dreams a reality. They eagerly try new techniques and philosophies that promise quick results. Some of these make a difference, but only for a while.

3. Preoccupied—Some people have achieved success as defined by our culture and still feel empty and unfulfilled.

   These people are highly motivated and see real results. They routinely set goals and achieve them. They have nice cars and a fine home, they take fantastic vacations, and they fill their lives with the fruit of their success. In the eyes of everyone watching, they've made it! But at some point, it's not enough to satisfy them. As the old adage goes, "People may spend their whole lives climbing the ladder of success only to find, once they reach the top, that the ladder is leaning against the wrong wall."[1] They measured up time after time, but they realized they'd been using the wrong yardstick.

   The poster child for this kind of person is, well, me. (I'll share more about myself a little later.)

4. Purposeful—Finally, some people connect both who they are and what they do to what matters most.

These people live with a clear sense of purpose, and nearly everything they do relates to it. Their passion is directed toward that purpose, and they have the energy and creativity to make it a reality. In fact, they live with a beautiful blend of drive and inner contentment while enjoying the journey of life. Successes are stepping stones to their ultimate end of making a difference in the lives of those around them. Setbacks don't destroy them, because they know they can learn valuable lessons from each failure that will fuel their next move. With this broader, deeper perspective, they realize all events, pleasant or painful, are neutral, and what matters is the meaning they give to each event. Success is just success, and failure is a gift because it's a chance to learn, grow, and begin again.

In all modesty this is who I've become, and it's the path many others have followed. This is the promise of The Results Tree.

In March of 2008 I was a major in the Air Force. My profession was navigating C-130s, large cargo legacy aircraft with four propellers, designed to transport troops and equipment in combat zones. After a number of deployments to South Central Asia, supporting the wars in Afghanistan and Iraq, I was selected to get a master's degree in foreign policy from the Naval Postgraduate School in Monterey, California. Years before, I graduated from the Air Force Academy and attended the Air Force Weapons School, our equivalent of the Navy TOPGUN school. After graduation I was asked to be one of the instructors. I had been very successful in the uncertainty of combat operations. My career was accelerating with momentum and promise.

It was an incredible honor to be a weapons officer. The Air Force describes the role this way:

> Weapons Officers . . . serve as advisors to military leaders at all levels, both those in uniform or in civilian government positions. [Weapons Officers] are the instructors of the Air Force's instructors and the service's institutional reservoir of tactical and operational knowledge. Taking the mantra, "humble, approachable and credible" as their creed, they form a band of trusted advisors and problem-solvers.[2]

While I was in Monterey, Jack, a lifelong friend who was one class ahead of me at the academy, called to ask if I wanted to attend a leadership training in Las Vegas. Instantly, I responded, "Vegas? Are you kidding? I'm in!"

My instant response was another example of my decision-making process: ready, fire, aim. I had agreed to something I knew nothing about and hadn't even asked a question about. I soon realized I'd signed up for emotional intelligence (EQ) training, which consisted of four days of exploring my current beliefs on who I was (with all the baggage from past hurts and failures and the misguided goals I was pursuing) and four days to examine what was holding me back from achieving my dreams.

After being involved in Weapons School, I didn't expect the leadership training to match its intensity. I was wrong. One of the exercises challenged us to wrestle with the fundamental question of identity (one that was far more challenging and impactful than I anticipated). The person asked repeatedly, "Who are you?" I mumbled some things that were superficial, but the question kept coming. I tried many different tactics to get the person to shut up, but she was relentless. Then it happened. Somehow the activity cut through years of building steel walls around my heart, and my deepest feeling about myself was suddenly exposed. I blurted out, "I don't love myself." I was startled. I said it again . . . and again. The realization hit me like a truck. I fell out of my chair onto the floor and wept uncontrollably. I had always been the cool guy, the one who had it all together, bulletproof, and always in command. In that instant, I knew I'd been living a lie.

Instantly, the blinders came off, and I realized this painful statement was the truest thing about me. While I was curled up in a ball on the floor, my life passed before me—the highs and the lows, the loves and the loneliness—and a clear pattern was revealed. As a result of my deep belief that I was unworthy and didn't deserve to be loved, I had sabotaged myself. Roughly every four years I blew up my career, my relationships, and my finances with the precision accuracy of a guided missile. *Blew up* is the right term. Let me describe five such instances, which I call bombs:

> **Bomb 1:** I nearly derailed my Air Force career before it ever had a chance to start. In the months leading up to my admission to the academy, I was arrested for stealing a pair of sunglasses from a discount store. I was able to have this violation offset with community service. Then, in the final weeks before admission to the academy I received a willful reckless-driving ticket.
>
> **Bomb 2:** At the academy I was the first cadet arrested for underage gambling. One weekend at a casino in Cripple Creek, Colorado, I sat for a few hands of blackjack. A policeman tapped me on the shoulder and asked for my ID. He didn't cite me. He just asked me to leave. I went down the street to another casino to play, and a few

minutes later the same policeman tapped me on the shoulder. This time, he took my chips and wrote a ticket.

Bomb 3: A few years later I was a lieutenant in flight school in San Antonio. I was invited to a wedding in Houston. While I was out with some buddies the night before the ceremony, I tossed a beer bottle that missed the trash can. I picked it up and put it away, but a policeman confronted me and demanded, "You need to leave the property." I started walking out, following the exit signs, but near the door, he grabbed me and sneered, "You have to leave the property right now!" At this point, it was just me and him. The rest of the guys were still in the club.

In a move that probably wasn't the smoothest, I said, "Then tell me where the property line is. Is the other side of the street OK?"

He snarled, "Why don't you wait in the street?"

Well, I wasn't going to take that, so I reached into my pocket for a scrap of paper and a pen and started writing his badge number. I put the paper and pen back into my pocket, and in a flash I was kissing the bricks! He threw me into the wall, handcuffed me, and escorted me to a lovely, all-expenses-paid overnight stay in the Harris County Jail. The next morning, my buddies posted bail right before I was to be arraigned. I left with them to drive back to San Antonio, but I had to return to court a couple of weeks later, which caused me to miss a day of flight school. I pleaded no contest and paid a fine. If I pleaded not guilty, I would have to return on a day when I was scheduled to fly, which couldn't be changed. And my commander told me that if I missed another day of training, he'd wash me out and I'd have to join the next class in flight school. I needed to fly that day to graduate.

Bomb 4: Years later, when I was stationed in Tokyo, I spent more time partying and chasing girls than flying airplanes. When the stint was over, I received a downgraded award that was a step below the exemplary medal others at my rank were awarded. It was the Air Force's way to place a black mark in my permanent record.

Bomb 5: When I was a teacher at the Weapons School, the cadre was developing call signs (nicknames) for the next class coming through, such as Maverick. That night, I went to a bar with the rest of our team. I bought shots for everybody. It was quite a party. Late that night, we piled into an SUV to return to base. I was in the rear cargo compartment. Before our designated driver drove off, a fight erupted outside the SUV. Bodies were smashing against the vehicle. It was a brawl, and it was reported to our commander that I'd invited our team to go that night. He was pissed. He demoted me from my position at the Weapons School and transferred me to a new unit. I had been at the pinnacle of the Air Force, and I'd blown it.

These weren't minor goofs. These were major conscious or subconscious efforts to undo years of hard work. I didn't see the pattern of achievement and sabotage, achievement and sabotage, over and over again. After each debacle, when I showed up at my next assignment, they assumed, "This guy is damaged goods. We'll see if he can cut it." And each time, I proved myself again. I did good work, impressed my commanders, and became indispensable, until the next explosion.

The message of hope I want to communicate is that despite all these debacles, I learned from the mistakes and crafted a clearer vision, reoriented my intentions, and chose more productive actions. Frankly, the pattern was undeniable once I had the courage to look and be honest with myself. It was against this backdrop that The Results Tree sprouted. The results are plain and monumental: a successful career in the Air Force, a loving and vibrant marriage, a beautiful family, a successful second career, fantastic friends, and on and on. These results are as much the product of God's grace and forgiveness as making better choices. The two aren't separated; they're inseparable, at least for me.

Verbalizing the painful truth, "I don't love myself," triggered a journey of self-discovery. I needed to figure out how that self-image had been shaped. I knew I needed to address the forces that had had such a powerful impact on me.

"You were not born to be average. You were born to be great. But greatness requires that you show up—even after failure."

ED MYLETT

I grew up in a little farming community in Nebraska, about ten miles from Lincoln, the state capital. Our family lived in what was once a Sears prefab house, shipped and assembled on-site. (Yes, they existed!) When I was seven years old, our family went out to eat at a restaurant in Lincoln. In the middle of the meal my dad got up and walked to the lobby to talk to a man. I could tell they were in a very important conversation, but I had no idea what it was about. I asked my mom who it was, and she told me, "It's the governor, Bob Kerry." I decided right there that my goal in life was to become governor of Nebraska, an ambition that had a domino effect on many subsequent choices.

I attended a very small high school of about one hundred students. One day during my sophomore year I walked into the school counselor's office (which was the size of a broom closet) and saw a catalog about the Air Force Academy. I read every word on every page. I was fascinated. By the time I put it down, I was completely hooked. There was no other place for me. I knew I needed to beef up what would go on my application, so I got involved in sports and competed in activities, including the Veterans of Foreign Wars Voice of Democracy and Boys'

State. I took a summer job working for the Gallup polling organization. I had a very clear vision that my future was to graduate from the academy and fly airplanes.

My high school graduating class had twenty students, sixteen of whom had been with me since kindergarten. I was laser focused on the Air Force Academy. It was the only school I applied to. I pushed all my chips to the middle of the table, but there was a problem. The admissions guide to the academy listed the minimum requirements for admission, but my ACT and SAT scores weren't good enough. I took them again, and again. I took the ACT four times and never got the qualifying score for English, but when I took the SAT a second time, I finally made the minimum score. I was relieved, until I got a letter from the academy stating that I hadn't been accepted for the class entering that fall that would graduate in 1995.[3]

When I got the rejection letter, I was heartbroken. A week or so later I received an offer for a scholarship from the Falcon Foundation, which provides resources for students who can't quite meet the academic requirements for the Air Force Academy but meet all the other admissions requirements. If I maintained a B average or better at a preparatory school, I would be admitted to the academy in the class of '96. I was at a disadvantage because other students had taken advanced-placement classes, while our little school offered simply math. No wonder I was behind. With the Falcon Foundation scholarship, I enrolled for the fall of '91 semester at the Marine Military Academy in Harlingen, Texas, down on the US-Mexican border. As it turned out, I would never make it to Harlingen.

Again, luck and God were on my side. On May 15, 1991, in my final days of high school, I was sitting in my American government class when the school secretary knocked on Mr. Hoyer's classroom door and asked to see me. She told me, "Senator Kerry is on the phone. He wants to talk to you." Bob Kerry, as you remember, was the governor my father had talked with years before, and now he was a US senator.

I went to the office, picked up the phone, and said, "Hello, Senator Kerry."

We chatted for a minute or two, and then he asked, "Gabriel, do you still want to go to the Air Force Academy?"

I almost shouted as I replied, "Yes sir!"

Without explanation he simply announced, "You're in. You need to be there on June 27."

I had plans for the summer, but they were thrown out the window in a flash. "I'll be there! Thank you, sir."

So on June 27, 1991, I entered the academy in the class of '95, honored to be one of only fifteen hundred cadets who passed the rigorous selection process. I was, and am, profoundly grateful to be able to live my dream, to be part of the long blue line, to have so many wonderful, dedicated friends, to receive worldclass education and training, and to wear our nation's uniform while serving in the war in Afghanistan and Iraq. At the time, I didn't know the terminology of The Results Tree, but on my journey to the academy, I lived the principles and practices of a *compelling vision, clear intentions, committed action,* and *results*.

My early history doesn't answer the question of where my self-image became one of self-hatred instead of self-acceptance. I know people who were abused as children, and I understand how they internalized the pain and fear. I know others who were abandoned, physically or emotionally, who have lived with the sense that they're unworthy of being loved. I see that clearly, but that's not my story. I believe we have a God-given internal compass, and if we aren't fixed on His love, forgiveness, and acceptance, we drift off course. As I grew up, I went to church regularly, but I believed success, pleasure, and approval were the chief aims of life, and everything I thought, said, and did revolved around those selfish pursuits. I was enrolled in pursuing fulfillment outside of myself, in an image, pretending to be someone I wasn't, for the sake of winning approval from friends, women, and colleagues. I was the epitome of the Rick Warren quote "We buy things we don't need with money we don't have to impress people we don't even know."[4] I wasn't a terrible person, and I wasn't the victim of terrible parents, but I had invested my life in less-than-productive pursuits.

Your backstory may be different. In fact, I'm sure it is in many ways. As I've spoken with men and women from all walks of life and all kinds of careers, I've found that many can still relate. That flash of insight, the realization that I didn't truly love myself, was both deeply painful and profoundly powerful. It became a turning point, one that redirected me toward a deeper sense of purpose.

The rest of this book is about the joy and fulfillment that come in finding a purpose far bigger than ourselves, one that brings out the very best in us, keeps us on track in the midst of difficulties and distractions, and produces life-changing results. Another way to say this is that the secret to a meaningful life lies in finding a new way to keep score. Life isn't about more, bigger, and better stuff; it's about more, bigger, and better impact on others. It's about living on purpose.

The Tree

Let me introduce you to the framework we'll use throughout the book and the exercises: The Results Tree.

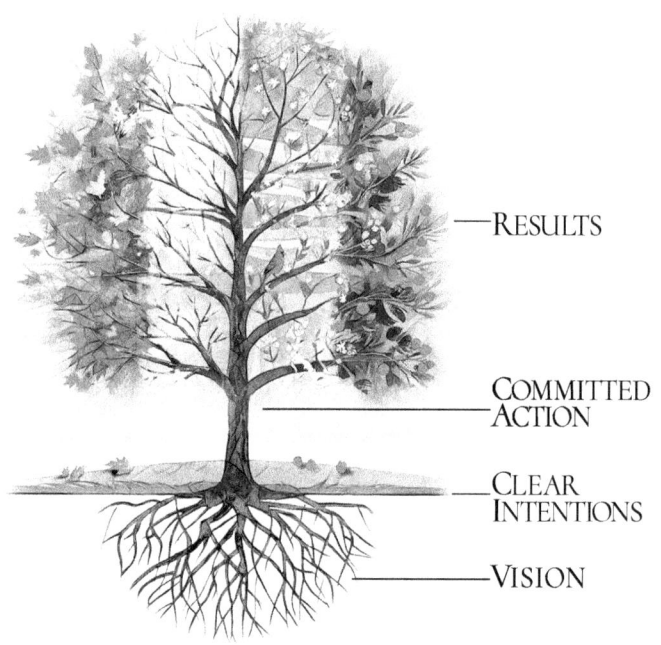

Vision

This is the million-dollar question: What do you want to be known for? What legacy do you hope to leave? What impact do you want to make on others? Your vision shapes everything. It fuels your choices, drives your behavior, and determines your results. It's not just a dream; it's your internal compass. Barring self-sabotage, your results will reflect the clarity and power of your vision. So ask yourself, "What is my unique *why*? What makes my mission personal, urgent, and worth making hard choices for every day?"

Clear Intentions

Your goals are how your vision takes shape. They bring it into the light and give it form. Here's the challenge: Too often our goals aren't truly connected to our deeper vision. We chase outcomes without anchoring them to purpose. When intentions are clear, we can own our goals so powerfully that they feel tangible. Clarity alone isn't enough. Clear intentions must be paired with committed action, accountability, and a deep emotional connection to why they matter, or they risk becoming just another checklist item or something we conveniently stop pursuing.

Committed Action

Clear intentions mark the starting line of real work. They're where action begins. In every moment, we face a choice. In time you will instinctively ask, "Does this action take me one step closer to my vision?" Committed action is fundamentally different from willpower. Willpower is about forcing it, white-knuckling, gritting your teeth, and pushing through. Committed action may look the same on the surface, but it's driven by purpose. It's rooted in your vision and fueled by passion. (We'll unpack this more in chapter 5, "Committed Action: Choose—Now!") At its core, committed action means choosing to show up, embrace what's difficult, and take deliberate steps that move your vision forward.

Results

Your results either will mirror your vision, clearly reflecting what you've intentionally set out to create, or will expose areas of misalignment. When outcomes fall short or take an unexpected turn, it is rarely random. More often this signals something deeper at work—an unconscious belief, a hidden fear, or a familiar pattern of self-sabotage. Just like the personal bombs I've shared or my struggle to love myself, these moments of misalignment are not failures; they are invitations. These moments are feedback from your inner world, pointing to the exact places where healing, realignment, or renewed intention is needed. Seen through this lens, misaligned results are not signs of defeat. They are markers showing you where to begin again, this time stronger, clearer, and more committed.

When alignment is present, when your Results Tree is producing good fruit, your outcomes will reflect the clarity of your intention and the depth of your committed action. The feedback becomes unmistakable, powerful, and deeply encouraging. You will witness the evidence of transformation, and that momentum will inspire you to keep moving forward. In those moments, resist the urge to rush ahead. Pause. Give thanks to God for His grace and guidance. Acknowledge the growth within yourself. Celebrate each step of progress, no matter how small. This act of gratitude not only honors the path you are on but also strengthens your identity as someone who walks in purpose, lives with clarity, and leads with resilience.

Choose Wisely

Many of us want guarantees. We hope life is like a vending machine: We put in our effort and we expect to get back the desired results. Life doesn't work that way, even for those of us who have the clearest vision and the strongest commitment to making good choices. Life happens.

An old story is told about a farmer in China who has a son about twenty years old. The farmer has a nice horse. One day a villager walks by and says, "You are a very lucky man to have such a fine horse."

The farmer smiles and says, "We'll see."

The next day, the horse runs away, and the villager tells the farmer, "Oh, such bad luck!"

The farmer responds, "We'll see."

Early the next morning, the horse returns with five more horses that had been part of a wild herd. The villager exclaims to the farmer, "You are so lucky!"

The farmer replies, "We'll see."

The next day, the farmer's son tries to break one of the wild horses, but he's thrown and breaks his leg. The villager shakes his head and moans, "That is terrible; you are so unlucky!"

The farmer says, "We'll see."

The next day, a general leads his army into the village and conscripts all the young men of fighting age, but when he sees the son's broken leg, he leaves him at home because he's unfit for military service. The villager walks by and sees this scene and remarks, "This is wonderful luck that your boy doesn't have to go to war!"

The farmer says, "We'll see."

The villager attached great significance to each event, but the farmer saw each one as neutral; he knew he didn't know (yet, at least) the meaning of each one. What this story teaches us is that events, in and of themselves, are neutral, and the personal meaning of any event is in a person's interpretation of it. This means we have a choice as to how we experience any event, and whether we attach a negative or positive meaning to it. For example, I can see a loss or a setback as evidence that I'm a failure, that I'll never succeed, or as a valuable learning opportunity that when applied will move me toward my goals.

Like the farmer, we need the wisdom to hold the future loosely in our hands while living in the present moment. Yes, we have a purpose, goals, and commitments, but there are no guarantees. People get sick, companies downsize, friends move away, children fall in with the wrong crowd, and those we love make self-destructive choices. If we believe the world (or a particular person or God) owes us a smooth ride to our carefully imagined destination, we're bound to be upset in two ways: We'll be upset when we experience troubles, and we'll be upset that we're upset about the troubles: "I shouldn't have to feel this way!"

One of the most important principles I've learned is that in every situation, *every* situation, I'm 100 percent responsible for how I respond. No matter what happens, I'm responsible for choosing to speak and act in a way that finds solutions and builds people up. With this perspective, there's no blaming, no scapegoating, no self-pity, and no catastrophizing. Every circumstance, pleasant or painful, is neutral and can be used for good. Always tell yourself this: "Events are neutral, and I'm always 100 percent responsible for how I respond."

Your Turn!

On first sight, Smokey triggered me. He had a very unique vibe, nothing like the straitlaced people all around me from my childhood and my military career. My wife, Kristie, and I were standing in the security line at an airport in Costa Rica. We had just arrived for a weeklong wellness retreat. He had long curly hair and was wearing beads and shorts. I walked away to pick up our bags, and when I returned, Smokey was chatting it up with Kristie. We walked through security and looked for our bus. Who was standing next to it? Smokey. He was going to the retreat too.

During the week, my defensiveness melted when I got to know him. I discovered he's an amazing person, a kind, loving, and devoted single dad raising two amazing sons. He's a hairstylist who has a genuine thirst for wisdom. His marriage didn't work out for him, but he didn't let that derail him.

The next year, Smokey missed the retreat. I called to find out what happened, and he told me he had contracted Bell's palsy, an unexplained muscle weakness or paralysis in the face, which often eventually goes away on its own.

The following year, Smokey's condition had improved enough for him to go on the retreat. When it was over, he was going through security at the Costa Rica airport and spotted a beautiful woman across the way out of thousands in the crowd. He pondered, "Why can't I find someone like that in Austin?" As the security line serpentined back and forth, they came face-to-face. He said hello and asked how her trip was. She said, "Amazing."

He ran into her again at the airport later, and he wondered why he couldn't stop thinking about her. She went up to him when he was sitting at a table alone and asked if she could join him. "Absolutely!" he responded. They learned they both lived in Austin. Then, he asked her where she was originally from, and she said Lubbock, Texas, which is where he was from! They also realized they had gone to the same high school, though they were a few years apart. It turned out she was on the same flight to Houston that day, so she saved a seat for him on the flight. After they landed, she asked him to join her and her kids for lunch. The two of them spoke for ten hours straight and felt a special connection. Today, they're still developing their relationship.

Smokey could have given up when he couldn't make the retreat because of Bell's palsy. Being delayed a year put him on the same flight with someone he almost certainly never would have met had the health problem not surfaced when it did. I can hear him say, "We'll see."

His story reminds me of the verse "And we know that God causes everything to work together for the good of those who love God and are called according to his purpose for them" (Romans 8:28, NLT).

No matter what our backgrounds are, no matter how many difficulties and traumas we've faced, it's possible to chart a new course aligned to our purpose.

More Than Willpower

I may not know you, but if you're like most people, I *know* you. You're always reaching, always striving, always trying as hard as you can. You've tried many techniques, many goal-setting plans, many, many times. You've mustered up enough willpower to keep going for a while (for some, a long, long while), but eventually, it wasn't enough. You quit. Willpower wasn't enough, again!

"You're never going to feel like it. Start anyway."
MEL ROBBINS

Certainly, there are moments when we need the willpower to press on, stay the course, and make hard decisions, but we need a better bedrock for our lives. We need our dream to be rooted in our vision. This is where we find sustained power. Willpower alone inevitably results in failure, guilt, shame, and utter exhaustion. It's because we are relying on manpower instead of God's power. It's not a workable way to live. Instead of depending on willpower, what will take you where you want to go is sinking your roots deep into a vision and purpose that capture your heart.

I'm offering an alternative. My hope is that the process I'm illustrating will give you such clarity about your vision and purpose that you'll wake up each day with a beautiful blend of drive and contentment. You'll see each day as a gift, and you'll see yourself as a gift to those around you. You'll be freed from the oppressive burden of *oughts* and *shoulds*. You'll find security, peace, and genuine joy, but you won't demand or expect any guarantees. Each day will be an adventure, another step or two on the path to having a purpose-driven impact on others. It's a journey. Enjoy it! In *Start with Why*, Simon Sinek remarks, "Very few people or companies can clearly articulate WHY they do WHAT they do. By WHY, I mean your purpose, cause, or belief—WHY does your company exist? WHY do you get out of bed every morning? And WHY should anyone care?"[5] When we can give clear and compelling answers to these questions, we're connected to our purpose, which fills us with passion and energy.

> *"For the Spirit God gave us does not make us timid, but gives us power, love and self-discipline."*
>
> 2 TIMOTHY 1:7

You've probably noticed that I've mentioned God, and you'll see references to Jesus Christ throughout this book. That's because my relationship with Christ is the foundation of my purpose, healing, and growth. I share my faith not to convince you but to be transparent about where my strength and direction come from. You may draw purpose from a different source, and that's completely OK. The principles, tools, and practices in *The Results Tree* are designed to be inclusive and impactful, no matter your background or beliefs. I occasionally reference the Bible, not as a requirement but because I've found timeless wisdom in its pages. Its teachings on things like integrity, love, forgiveness, and discipline echo through many of the world's great traditions and philosophies. If faith isn't your lens, that's fine. The power of intentional living and transformation is universal.

At the heart of that transformation is choice. Every moment offers one. In *The Matrix*, Neo is presented with a defining decision: take the red pill and face the hard truth, or take the blue pill and remain in the comfort of illusion. It's a cinematic metaphor, but also a daily reality. Growth often requires us to confront uncomfortable truths. When that moment comes, you may feel fear, anxiety, or doubt. Those emotions are natural. They're also data. Emotions are energy in motion, signaling opportunities for insight and realignment. We can suppress them, or we can engage with them. Avoidance may offer temporary relief, but unexperienced emotions eventually surface in ways that cause harm, to ourselves and others. Choosing to feel, learn, and grow takes courage, and it's how we become whole.

In his book *Healing the Shame That Binds You*, John Bradshaw shares, "Underneath the mask of adult behavior there is a child who was neglected. This needy child is insatiable. What that means is that when the child becomes an adult, there is a 'hole in his soul.'"[6] Take the red pill. You may not like it at first, but it will cause you to grow wiser and stronger, and it just might save your life.

As you read this book and work through the exercises, find the courage to tackle what's hard for you. That's where you'll find the most valuable growth. And remember, the shortest route to your destination is through, not around.

Now let's dive into the first exercises.

 I'd love to walk with you on this journey. Check out The Results Tree Experience eCourse, where I'll guide you step-by-step as you put this framework into practice and move from insight to action.

EXERCISES
A Different Angle

When you think of *paralyzed, plagued, preoccupied,* or *purposeful*, which of these best describes you at this moment? Explain your answer.

_____
_____
_____

What are some bombs you've detonated in your life, times when you did something to sabotage yourself, damage your own self-esteem and self-worth, and limit the opportunities available?

_____
_____
_____

What difference would it make to see these and other failures and mistakes as neutral events you can learn from?

_____
_____
_____

As you think about the self-analysis required to benefit from The Results Tree, are you reaching for the red pill of reality or the blue pill of willful ignorance?

_____
_____
_____

What would truly forgiving yourself look like? Are you willing to forgive? Are you ready to let go of the old stories and the old you?

_____

_____

_____

"Knowing yourself is the beginning of all wisdom."
ARISTOTLE

Chapter 2

VISION
The Necessary Roots

It is not about you. The purpose of your life is far greater than your own personal fulfillment, your peace of mind, or even your happiness. It is far greater than your family, your career, or even your wildest dreams and ambitions.
RICK WARREN

Far too often we look for meaning in the wrong places. Finding an authentic purpose in life means digging down deep into the rich soil of our culture's crying needs and big opportunities. Mitch Albom, the author of *Tuesdays with Morrie*, has the main character, Morrie, give this advice: "The way you get meaning into your life is to devote yourself to loving others, devote yourself to your community around you, and devote yourself to creating something that gives you purpose and meaning."[7]

A friend who lives on the Gulf Coast has been through a number of tropical storms and hurricanes. He marveled that through all these storms, he's never seen a live oak tree uprooted and toppled. "But an

————VISION

ash tree fell before the high winds even reached us." I asked him to explain the difference. "Simple," he smiled, and said, "The tree that fell had very shallow roots, but live oaks have a really strong root system. It's hard to get oaks up even with a bulldozer!"

So, which are you? Our ability to weather life's inevitable storms is directly related to the strength of our root system. Our personal dream, our life vision, is our root system. (I use the terms *dream* and *vision* interchangeably.) A strong root system provides both stability and nourishment. With it we persevere and thrive through hard times; without it we waver and collapse.

Someone once asked me, "Gabriel, how did you decide on the vision for your life?"

After reflecting for a moment, I explained, "I didn't decide on it. It was already there. I just got to uncover it, name it, validate it, and learn how to connect every moment of every day to it." Too many of us feel confused because others have told us what our dream ought to be, but a borrowed dream isn't our own. We need one that comes from within.

It seems that children are more in touch with their dreams than most adults. A six-year-old lives to play with trucks, learn about dinosaurs or sharks, have a family of dolls, or play baseball in the backyard with an older sibling. They aren't confused, and they don't struggle with what matters most to them. They're naturally curious and creative. When my oldest, Preston, was younger, he loved riding his bike. My friend Daniel taught him to ride in a single afternoon, and from that moment, he jumped on his bike whenever he had a few minutes. My daughter Mikayla, who goes by MG, loves rainbows and unicorns and preferably rainbow unicorns. When we played twenty questions, her secret was always a dead giveaway: a rainbow unicorn. She had them on her pillows and sheets, her backpack, binders, posters, books, you name it. When teachers gave her art assignments, she never used the full spectrum of colors. If she drew the Rocky Mountains, they were pink and purple, with a prominent horn somewhere among the peaks. Harrison has always been fascinated with snakes and lizards. It must be recessive genes because Kristie and I have not yet learned how to love reptiles! Harrison knows every kind of snake and catches the nonpoisonous ones with his bare hands.

Kristie and I didn't sit each of them down and try to help them determine what captured their hearts. It was already there. Our pleasant task was to affirm it and provide the resources for them to explore what they loved.

So why is it so hard for many of us to identify our dreams? What's the cost of trying to live by one we've borrowed from someone else? And what's the steeper cost of not having one at all? Some of us have read so many books, attended so many seminars, and heard from so many friends about the vision for their lives that we've tried hard to draw a little from each of them, and it's a mess. Our vision statements sound like Frankenstein, a bunch of random parts glued and sewn together into something awkward and unrecognizable. And worse, it doesn't express what's authentically meaningful and important to us.

The one I've uncovered and identified (and clarified several times over the years) is "I live grounded in faith, creating epic experiences." Those epic experiences are for me, my family, and those I come in contact with every day in person, through *The Navigating Leaders Podcast*, or through this book. This encapsulates my deepest desires, taps into my heartfelt passion, and brings forth my best talents. My vision is that this book will be an epic experience for you.

Two Ways to Live

All of us are radically affected by our culture. It's the air we breathe and the water we swim in. Consumerism promises fulfillment, but it satisfies only for a moment. Then we need the next gadget, the better vacation, the latest car, or a new spouse who loves us the way we want to be loved. The thirst for more is baked into our society. Think about commercials. They're designed to create discontent; that's how they lure us to buy the product or service. Social media operates in the same way, promising meaning but using algorithms to tap into anger, resentment, and the relentless desire for more. An article in *Harvard*

Business Review reports recent studies in "neuromarketing," using the science of the brain to manipulate consumers.[8] The ads we see on television or online aren't haphazard attempts to get our attention; they're carefully calculated to arouse our primal brains to take decisive action to buy products, enlist services, or be committed to a cause.

Decades ago, during the Great Depression, people were thrilled just to put food on the table. They weren't obsessed with always needing more. However, when the country became more prosperous, Ernest Dichter came up with a solution to drive higher sales. His company, Motivational Research, shifted the focus of advertising from the qualities of the product to the wants of the consumer. Toothpaste not only cleans your teeth; the new wave of advertising promises that toothpaste will make you popular, beautiful, and irresistible! Today, virtually every ad contains this secondary, and far more powerful, incitement to buy. Daniel Yankelovich wrote *New Rules* to describe how our culture has moved from *self-sacrifice* before and during World War II to *self-indulgence* now. In a scathing indictment of our culture, Charles J. Sykes wrote *A Nation of Victims: The Decay of the American Character*. He describes how our culture's focus on personal rights has slipped into selfishness, self-pity, and the use of litigation as a tool to get what we demand. A friend of mine once pointed out that where there are rights, there is also responsibility. The two cannot be separated.

To get what we demand—that's the point. People have always been self-focused, but today, it's on steroids! If we look closely, we'll see two very different ways to live.

HAVE-DO-BE

The way most of us approach life can be described as have-do-be: We believe that if we have enough possessions, popularity, and pleasure, we'll impress people with how we look, what we are doing, and where we go. Then we'll be truly happy and fulfilled. To get these things, we devote our time and talents to earning enough money and pleasing the right people. If and when we have enough, we think, we can finally be free and enjoy life. But how much is enough?

> *"The two most important days in your life are the day you are born and the day you find out why."*
>
> MARK TWAIN

People who live this way are pawns in the game of comparison and competition. Their sense of self-worth is entirely determined by external criteria—more success, pleasure, and approval than before, and more than the other people in their sphere of friendships. They vacillate from day to day, and sometimes from moment to moment, between feelings of superiority (when they're doing better than someone else) and feelings of inferiority (when they're not). Pride and fear are constant companions. In his seminal work, *Mere Christianity*, C. S. Lewis commented, "Pride gets no pleasure out of having something, only out of having more of it than the next [person]. . . . It is the comparison that makes you proud: the pleasure of being above the rest. Once the element of competition is gone, pride is gone."[9] In the same vein, Theodore Roosevelt observed, "Comparison is the thief of joy."[10]

Ninety-nine people out of a hundred live by have-do-be, and as a result, no matter how much success they experience, satisfaction is fleeting. Let me give two examples. Tom Brady is known as the GOAT. He led the New England Patriots to six Super Bowl championships and was named the league's MVP three times. He's handsome and articulate, was married to a supermodel, and has made tens of millions in salary and endorsements. His teammates love him because he took a lower pay so the team could afford other skilled players on the free-agent market. He often included his offensive linemen in endorsement deals so they could share the wealth. Could life be any better than that? In an interview on 60 *Minutes* after the third championship, Brady discussed the stresses caused by his fame. All the money and fame, he explained, left him feeling confused and empty. He complained, "Why do I have three Super Bowl rings and still think there's something greater out there for me?" He mused that he had reached his highest goals and had every desire fulfilled, but he reflected sadly, "God, it's got to be more than this!"[11]

The interviewer asked, "What's the answer?"

Brady laughed. "I wish I knew. I love playing football, and I love being the quarterback for this team. But at the same time, there are a lot of other parts about me that I'm trying to find."[12]

He learned (the hard way) that our deep longing for meaning, for self-love, will never be fulfilled by external things.

Similarly, Taylor Swift is one of the most successful musical artists of her generation. She has dominated charts, won countless awards, and influenced a global fan base. But even at the height of fame she struggled with internal pressure and fear of inadequacy. In her documentary *Miss Americana*, she admitted, "My entire moral code, as a kid and now, is a need to be thought of as good.... It was all I wrote about; it was all I wanted, to be seen as good." She went on to reveal how deeply her identity had become tied to approval and achievement.

At one point Swift confessed, "You're always balancing, or trying to balance, the feeling of 'I'm not enough' with the feeling of 'I'm too much.'" Despite her public success, she described feeling trapped by the need to constantly prove herself, living for the next round of applause to confirm she was still relevant, still valuable.[13]

Her words echo the same inner conflict Tom Brady once described, a quiet discontent beneath the surface of outward success.

Both point to a profound truth: No level of external success, no amount of achievement, recognition, or material gain, can truly satisfy the deeper longing for identity, self-worth, and inner peace. If I don't love and value myself just as I am, if I don't believe I'm worthy and enough without the trophies, then nothing I gain will ever feel like enough. Real healing happens in quieter places, away from the spotlight, where we confront the wounds to our self-esteem, often carried from childhood, and begin to repair our sense of worth. When my happiness, purpose, and fulfillment are no longer dependent on what I achieve or accumulate, I can live with freedom. I can be fully present in the now, aligned with my deepest values and vision. This is the essence of living from the inside out, from be-do-have. Who I am (be) shapes what I do, and what I do shapes what I have. Great relationships, impactful work, even peace of mind all begin with who I am and who I am becoming.

God has made us so that we're only truly fulfilled when our hearts are in tune with Him and His priorities. When external success, fame, money, and all the things money can buy take God's place in the center of our affections, the fabric of God's design for us is torn, and we suffer the consequences.

We can identify many counterfeits of ultimate purpose. They include:

- Power: "My life has meaning, and I have worth only if I have power and influence over others." If this is what motivates you and has captured your heart, you dread being humiliated, people around you often feel used, and your common emotion is anger.
- Approval: "My life has meaning, and I have worth only if I'm loved and respected by certain others." If this is what motivates you and captures your heart, your great fear is rejection. People often feel that you smother them, and you're a coward when others need to be told hard truths. In *Daring Greatly*, Brené Brown describes the difference between truly belonging and desperately seeking acceptance. We can be known and loved only if we take off the masks we wear to impress people. She explains, "Belonging is the innate human desire to be part of something larger than us. Because this yearning is so primal, we often try to acquire it by fitting in and by seeking approval, which are not only hollow substitutes for belonging but often barriers to it. Because true belonging only happens when we present our authentic, imperfect selves to the world, our sense of belonging can never be greater than our level of self-acceptance."[14]
- Comfort: "My life has meaning, and I have worth only if I'm free from hassles and experience uninterrupted pleasure." If this is what motivates you and captures your heart, you're afraid of people putting too many demands on you, and others feel neglected because you're so self-absorbed and afraid of being bored.
- Control: "My life has meaning, and I have worth only if I master my craft, spouse, kids, community, hobbies . . . I have control of the

process." If this is your motivation and what captures your heart, you feel the need to always call the shots, and more importantly, you are terrified of being out of control. You're afraid of uncertainty and loose ends, others often feel condemned because they don't measure up to your impossibly high standards, and a constant struggle is worry.[15]

These four are just a few of many counterfeits, but they're probably the most common. Novelist David Foster Wallace compared our devotion to externals to worship. In a commencement speech at Kenyon College he told the audience:

> If you worship money and things—if they are where you tap real meaning in life—then you will never have enough. Never feel you have enough. It's the truth. Worship your own body and beauty and sexual allure and you will always feel ugly, and when time and age start showing, you will die a million deaths before they finally plant you. On one level, we all know this stuff already—it's been codified as myths, proverbs, clichés, bromides, epigrams, parables: the skeleton of every great story. The trick is keeping the truth up front in daily consciousness. Worship power—you will feel weak and afraid, and you will need ever more power over others to keep the fear at bay. Worship your intellect, being seen as smart—you will end up feeling stupid, a fraud, always on the verge of being found out.[16]

Was calling these pursuits "worship" overstatement? No, not in my experience. Worship means we consider something to be worthy. When we worship, we're saying that person, experience, or thing is supremely valuable to us, and we're committed to protecting, defending, and advancing it. We're pledging our loyalty to it. Isn't that what Wallace was talking about? Things such as beauty and power and intellect aren't wrong or evil, but they're secondary. Two passages in Jeremiah illustrate this point. In the second chapter God speaks to His people:

> My people have exchanged their glorious God for worthless idols.... My people have committed two sins: They have forsaken me, the spring of living water, and have dug their own cisterns, broken cisterns that cannot hold water.
> —JEREMIAH 2:11, 13

God was saying, "Why do you look for meaning and fulfillment from things that can't deliver? Come to Me."

Being thirsty is a common metaphor for the desire for ultimate meaning. Jesus stood up at a great feast in Jerusalem and cried out, "Let anyone who is thirsty come to me and drink. Whoever believes in me, as Scripture has said, rivers of living water will flow from within them" (John 7:37–38). Are we thirsty for meaning and belonging? Absolutely. Through Jeremiah, God said His people weren't drinking from the fountain of living water. Instead, they dug cisterns that were broken and leaked.

Later in Jeremiah, God's message parallels Wallace's, but He adds the remedy:

> "Let not the wise boast of their wisdom or the strong boast of their strength or the rich boast of their riches, but let the one who boasts boast about this: that they have the understanding to know me, that I am the Lord, who exercises kindness, justice and righteousness on earth, for in these I delight," declares the Lord.
> —JEREMIAH 9:23–24

A boast shows something we believe in, something we count on, something of surpassing importance. It's entirely common for smart people to depend on their intelligence as the source of their security and importance, for powerful people to rely on their strength, and for rich people to put their hopes in their financial security, but God says there's something, actually Someone, far more secure and valuable: His kindness, justice, and righteousness, and the amazing fact that we can know Him, and it's always and only by His grace.

What are you looking for today to quench your thirst?

I want to stop for a moment and address a concern you may have. I'm sharing the perspective that has been and is very meaningful to me. My relationship with God gives me both security and purpose. I'm still a work in progress, but my experience of God's love and forgiveness lowers my anxiety level, and the Bible points me to a purpose far bigger than myself. If you're resistant to what I am sharing, I invite you to take on the principles and practices of The Results Tree and find security and purpose in your own way. I hope sharing about my faith encourages you to examine the hope I've found in Christ, but if it turns you off, find a different source of security and purpose, and please keep reading.

New York Times columnist David Brooks observes that the philosophers who shaped Western culture assume people are fundamentally selfish, and Western economic theory is based on the self-interested pursuit of wealth and power. Brooks, however, disagrees:

> But this worldview is clearly wrong. In real life, the push of selfishness is matched by the pull of empathy and altruism. This is not Hallmark Channel sentimentalism but scientific fact: As babies, our neural connections are built by love and care. We have evolved to be really good at cooperation and empathy. We are strongly motivated to teach and help others.

There are, Brooks, asserts, "two lenses" people use to view poverty and prosperity: the economic lens or the moral lens. When people are motivated primarily for financial gain, they fail to follow "their natural bias toward reciprocity, service and cooperation." He draws a stark contrast between other-focused and self-focused cost-benefit calculus. He concludes:

> To be a good citizen, to be a good worker, you often have to make an altruistic commitment to some group or ideal, which will see you through those times when your job of citizenship is hard and frustrating. Whether you are a teacher serving students or a soldier serving your country or a clerk who likes your office mates, the moral motivation is much more powerful than the financial motivations. Arrangements that arouse the financial lens alone are just messing everything up.[17]

In combat, when bullets are flying and artillery shells are exploding all around, soldiers seldom think about the issues that started the war. Instead, they fight for the people on their right and left. A Civil War veteran explained, "When the chips are down, the man fights to help the man next to him. Men do not fight for a cause, but because they do not want to let their comrades down."[18] Later, in World War I, "soldiers had to charge out of the trenches and across no-man's land into a hail of bullets and shrapnel and poison gas. They were easy targets and casualties were enormously high."[19] When asked why, these soldiers often shared they didn't want to let their fellow soldiers down, to be cowards. So they did the unthinkable and charged forward.

What do you want to be known for, looking out for yourself or what you contributed to others?

Be-Do-Have

Most people go through life following a simple but deceptive formula: *Have-Do-Be*. Once I *have* enough money, love, approval, or success, then I'll *do* what I really want—travel, write, rest, give—and finally I'll *be* happy, fulfilled, confident, or whole. That formula rarely delivers what it promises. When we build our identity on what we *have*, our foundation becomes fragile. One market crash, one failed relationship, or one health scare, and we're right back to questioning our worth. To put it another way, when I base my happiness and fulfillment on temporary things, then, at best, my happiness or fulfillment can only be temporary.

There is a better way. A more grounded, authentic, and powerful approach: *Be-Do-Have*. When we begin by deciding who we want to *Be*—a generous leader, a present parent, a courageous friend—we act from that identity, rather than chasing external validation. This inner clarity naturally shapes our actions (*Do*) and the outcomes we experience (*Have*). Living from *Be-Do-Have* isn't just about achieving goals; it's about cultivating integrity, joy, and peace regardless of circumstances. It allows you to live with wholeness, rather than constantly striving for it.

Our sense of identity, our *being*, is what ultimately drives the choices we make and the lives we build. Most of us spend years chasing status, achievements, accolades, or possessions, hoping they'll offer the security and significance we crave. But they can't. Whether we can articulate it or not, our deepest longing is to be fully known and deeply loved, not one or the other but both. If someone knows everything about us but doesn't love us, it's terrifying. If someone says they love us but doesn't really know us, it feels hollow.

So where do we find that kind of security? Some of us experienced glimpses of it as children, perhaps through "good enough" parents who made us feel protected, nurtured, and delighted in. When that happens, we internalize the message that we have intrinsic value. The roots of self-worth grow deep, and it's easier to believe that a loving God cherishes us.

I'm deeply grateful for the foundation my parents, church, and community helped build in me. Many grew up in very different environments, homes marked by chaos, addiction, abuse, abandonment, or emotional distance. For some, security was shattered like a bottle against concrete. Others endured constant criticism, like sandpaper on their soul. When affection and affirmation were scarce, it was hard to believe we were lovable at all.

To survive, many of us learned to compensate: pleasing others to earn approval, achieving to prove our worth, or hiding to avoid expectations. Does any of that sound familiar?

The message of the Bible is that each of us is so valuable to God that He made the most astounding sacrifice to demonstrate His love and welcome us home. Jesus took the judgment we deserved so we could receive the honor and affection He deserves. It's the great exchange, grace in its purest form.

Author Paul David Tripp defines *grace* this way: It is "freely-given love, forgiveness, acceptance, and help of God." He further explains:

> You need it. You can't live without it, but you can't purchase it and you can't earn it. It only ever comes by means of a gift, and when you receive it, you immediately realize how much you needed it all along, and you wonder how you could've lived so long without it.
>
> In a fallen world populated by selfish, lost, fearful, and rebellious people, it's the one thing that everyone needs. And you can only give it to someone else when you have first been given it yourself because you can't give away that which you don't have.

> You see, God's grace is the most powerful force in the universe, so I would have to argue that it's the most beautiful word in the universe. It reaches you where you are and takes you where God has designed you to be. It has the power to do something that nothing else can do: transform you at the causal core of who you are as a human being—your heart.[20]

The experience of grace is how you grow roots like a live oak. It delights you that the most important Being in the universe is crazy about you, gives you freedom to be creative because you're not afraid of failure, connects you with people who have found the same freedom and creativity, and invites you to dream of having a far greater impact. Grace fertilizes the roots of your vision and gives you the courage to be curious and dare greatly.

One of the most perplexing things Jesus said was that to be fulfilled, we need to "die to self." In a world that elevates success, pleasure, and approval above all else, His directive seems counterintuitive, yet it holds the secret to unlocking purpose, joy, and wholeness. My wife, Kristie, shared it best: "Dying to self and surrendering to God's purpose for my life was simple. I was the one making it hard. Now it's a day-by-day, sometimes even minute-by-minute, commitment to stay in His will. When I live in this space, I surrender control and step into the flow with God. It's magical, and once experienced, I never want to be separated from Him. From this place, I get to give myself grace so I can give grace to others, remembering that surrender is not weakness but the doorway to freedom."

We start the process of spiritual formation from a point of ambiguity. We're complex creatures, full of the capacity for goodness but often controlled by selfish desires, deeply loved by God yet terribly flawed. It's important to keep both in mind. If we forget that we're created in the image of God, we can live under the crushing weight of shame, fear, and doubt. Or if we forget that our motivations are never completely pure, we'll be arrogant and use people instead of loving them. In one of Philip Yancey's books, he quotes a Jewish rabbi: "A man should carry two stones in his pocket. On one should be inscribed, 'I am but dust and ashes.' On the other, 'For my sake the world was created.' And he should use each stone as he needs it."[21] Those who expect everything to go smoothly will be disappointed. The secret is to fall in love with the journey, one that sometimes leads to mountain peaks with gorgeous vistas but occasionally leads through dark swamps when you feel lost. People who are successful but empty live for the mountaintops; those who are bored or anxious worry they'll never get out of the swamp. A grounded person develops perception, patience, and wisdom.

Wisdom enables me to own my failures. They don't define me; they don't condemn me; they don't threaten me; they're just a classroom where I can learn important lessons and move on. Some of us catastrophize, blowing up every minor error into a nuclear explosion! And when the explosion is seemingly over, it's still not over. We relive it a dozen times, beating ourselves up for being so stupid. Others minimize ("It wasn't that bad."), excuse ("Hey, it wasn't my fault!"), or deny ("What problem? I don't see a problem."). I'll never learn from a mistake if I don't own it.

All successes and failures are classrooms. The event itself is neutral, neither good nor bad. When I'm secure and grounded, I have that perspective, and a door to living The Results Tree opens.

And it's all based on owning: I am 100 percent responsible.

EVOLUTION OF A VISION

My vision for my life has changed over time. It hasn't changed from one thing to another, but it has become clearer and more concise. Nearly twenty years ago my professional coach, Stacy James, gave me the assignment of writing a vision statement. After a lot of soul-searching I came up with this: "Living responsibly and standing for humanity in their responsibility." Based on my early years, you can understand why responsibility was a thing for me. A few years later I refined my vision and wrote this: "Living grounded in faith, creating epic experiences."

"The only thing worse than being blind is having sight but no vision."
HELEN KELLER

As I told a friend about this progression, he asked, "OK, what was it before Stacy gave you the assignment? What was your vision twenty-five years ago?"

I answered, "Twenty-five years ago my vision wasn't clear to my conscious mind, but I believe it was already etched into my subconscious and on my heart. I was living like a rabid consumer, treating everything, and everyone, as a commodity. I lacked the self-accountability and responsibility I needed to actually live out my true purpose. Looking back, I think I inched closer to my vision through a long series of missteps, actions and decisions that simply weren't working for my good. Each failure was a clue. Each consequence, a breadcrumb. And slowly, I started to recognize that what I really wanted wasn't more but something deeper, something aligned." Notice that my vision became more and more clear as I examined the Results I was creating in my life.

INSIDE OUT OR OUTSIDE IN

The first three kinds of people, those who are stuck, distressed, or empty, usually have dreams focused on externals and a vision that came from someone or somewhere else. No matter how much they achieve or how much they blame themselves or others for their lack of achievement, they live with a nagging sense that life isn't working. Even for successful people, living under intense pressure to perform better than the people around us may stimulate a lot of activity, but it robs us of joy, peace, and real satisfaction.

Make no mistake, each of us has an insatiable desire, a real need, to fill the hole in our hearts. If we feel bored, distressed, or empty, we'll look for external things—people, possessions, and projects—to fill us. If we're honest with ourselves, we realize we're using every available resource to fill the hole. We may be kind or brutal, driven or passive, but our ultimate aim is to quiet the nagging voice of emptiness. However, when we feel known and loved, the hole is filled and overflowing. We have an abundant amount to give, and our vision, goals, and activities become more outward-focused. It works like this:

» Loved people love people, even unlovely people.
» Forgiven people forgive people, even those who have hurt them.
» Accepted people accept people, even those who are different.
» Graced people show grace to others.
» Healed people heal people, even those who feel hopeless.

Or, as Barack Obama said, "*Change* will not come if we wait for some other person or some other time. We are the ones we've been waiting for. We are the *change* that we seek."[22]

It's that simple. It's that powerful. Don't miss it.

The point is that we need a vision that's far bigger than the acquisition of things, pats on the back, or awards on a wall. Don't get me wrong, I sure like these three things. They promise to give us ultimate fulfillment, wholeness, and purpose, but they can't, and won't. We need something transcendent. I believe the Christian faith calls us to a purpose that takes us out of our small, selfish world and transports us to a vision of making a difference in the lives of others. In his book *The Call*, Os Guinness writes, "Calling is the truth that God calls us to himself so decisively that everything we are, everything we do, and everything we have is invested with a special devotion and dynamism lived out as a response to his summons and service."[23] Everything—seriously, everything.

What does it look like for you and me? That's part of the adventure. There are common characteristics of compassion, service, creativity, and tenacity, but the exact outlines are unique to each person. For me (and many others), Jesus provides a purpose far bigger than myself—to bring His kingdom of love and strength into every activity and relationship—an example to follow and plenty of motivation to pursue it. If you find a transcendent purpose through some other religion or philosophy, great, go for it, but don't settle for anything less than a vision you're willing to die for.

We have to be careful, though, to be sure that our kindness and generosity are actually helping people. I heard a story about four investment bankers who went on an annual fishing trip to Tahiti. Each year, they stayed in the same huts on the beach and hired the same guide. They had a great time every year. After they'd been going for more than a decade, one of them said, "Why don't we offer to help this guy?"

The others thought it was a good idea, so after a day of fishing, they asked the guide, "How many trips like this do you do each year?"

He looked perplexed and said, "About one group a week, usually for five days. They often leave things behind they'd bought just for the trip, so we get paid and get some cool things too."

"Great," one of the investment bankers replied. "Let's figure out your revenue stream, expenses, and net profits."

The guide looked even more confused. He asked, "Why would I do that?"

Each of the four jumped in with all the reasons a good business plan would help him. At the end of the list, one of them said, "And if you save enough money, you can retire!" He was sure that sealed the deal.

Another banker saw that the guide wasn't convinced, so he chimed in: "You could raise your rates 10 percent and put the extra income in a mutual fund. Before long you'd have quite a lot of money."

The guide asked, "Why would I do that?"

One of them burst in, "So you can do what you really want to do!"

After a few seconds the guide smiled and said, "I really want to take people fishing." He paused for a second and then laughed as he told them, "I guess that means I'm already retired!"

The four bankers thought they were helping and offering much-needed advice, but they didn't include a vital element: listening. Find someone who will listen to you to clarify your vision. And if someone is trying to identify a vision, ask good questions and listen carefully. The vision may be hidden, but it will be gradually revealed.

Your Vision

In the past few years I've become more aware of the need for and the power of curiosity. Children are naturally curious, with an insatiable desire to explore and know more. As adults it takes intention, time, and courage to be curious. This creative process is the heartbeat of all discoveries, in science, medicine, music, arts, technology, and the human heart.

Don't rush through this part of life. The journey is the most important part! Wrestle with it; dig deep into what matters to you. The bankers didn't take time to listen to the guide's dreams. They didn't realize he was already living his dream and fulfilling his purpose. They made assumptions, and they missed what he was saying completely. Take time to listen to your heart. If a compelling vision statement doesn't appear on your paper right away, it's no big deal. Mine took time to be revealed, and it has evolved over time, but each iteration has captured a little more of what God has put on my heart to be, to do, and to have.

> *"Pain pushes until vision pulls."*
> DR. MICHAEL B. BECKWITH

Do you want to make a difference? Be a servant leader, no matter what your career may be. The term was first coined by Robert Greenleaf in his 1970 essay "The Servant as Leader." He explains:

> The servant-leader is a servant first. . . . It begins with the natural feeling that one wants to serve, to serve first. Then conscious choice brings one to aspire to lead. That person is sharply different from one who is a leader first, perhaps because of the need to assuage an unusual power drive or to acquire material possessions. For such it will be a later choice to serve—after leadership is established. The leader-first and the servant-first are two extreme types. Between them there are shadings and blends that are part of the infinite variety of human nature.

To Greenleaf the outcomes of the two forms of leadership are clear. His series of questions sharpens the contrasts:

> The difference manifests itself in the care taken by the servant-first leader to make sure that the other people's highest priority needs are being served. The best test, and difficult to administer, is: Do those served grow as persons? Do they, while being served, become healthier, wiser, freer, more autonomous, more likely themselves to become

servants? And, what is the effect on the least privileged in society; will they benefit, or, at least, not be further deprived?[24]

Servant leaders have grasped "the upside-down principle at the heart of the universe":

- » The last shall be first, and the first shall be last.
- » To have true riches, give generously.
- » To have real power, give it away.
- » If we try to save our lives, we'll lose them, but if we lose our lives for others, we'll find them.
- » To experience the relief of forgiveness, we get to forgive others and ourselves.
- » The proud will be humbled, and the humble will be exalted.[25]

In *Leaders Eat Last*, Simon Sinek observes, "The true price of leadership is the willingness to place the needs of others above your own."[26]

People who live this way are rare and inspiring. We need more of them. Will you be one?

Insecure people aren't humble. They present themselves as either dominant, overly eager to please, or disengaged, entirely avoiding challenging people and situations. We might mistake the person who "reads the room" and adjusts to gain approval as humble, but more often than not, they're driven by fear: fear of not being enough, of not being lovable. Their people-pleasing is a strategy to earn worth. Likewise, those who try to disappear into the background may appear modest, but they're often doing so from a place of deep self-doubt, insignificance, or anger.

Humility is living, giving, and receiving from an accurate and authentic sense of self not inflated by pride or diminished by shame. It's the quiet confidence of knowing who you are and what you're not, and being at peace with both. Humility isn't passivity; in fact, it takes tremendous strength to function at a high level without needing attention or recognition from others. It allows you to show up, stand firm, and serve meaningfully, not to impress or escape but simply because it aligns with who you are.

A powerful vision is not about dominating others, pleasing them to win acceptance, or hiding to avoid rejection. It's about knowing who you are and living from that deep center with courage, clarity, and compassion.

As our vision takes shape, we'll spend time fine-tuning it. In his book *Visioneering*, Andy Stanley insists: "If it's not memorable, it's not portable." It's far better for a leader's vision to be incomplete yet memorable than to be carefully thought through but thoroughly forgettable. He explains:

> [If] it doesn't roll off the tip of your tongue, it's not easy to integrate into a conversation.... For vision to stick it's got to be stated simply, simply, simply, simply. This is difficult and here's part of the reason why. Some of you will really struggle with this. In order to make your vision simple it can't be complete. That means you've got to leave some stuff out.... It'll be accurate, but nobody's going to know what it is. You've got to make the decision: Do we want to make it portable and transferable, and do we want to make it stick? Or do we want it to be ... correct and accurately complete but nobody's going to know what it is?[27]

Writing focuses the mind and helps clear out the fog of uncertainty. In a time of anxiety and confusion for the people of Israel, God told His prophet,

> Write down the vision and inscribe it clearly on tablets, so that one who reads it may run. For the vision is yet for the appointed time; it hurries toward the goal and it will not fail. Though it delays, wait for it; for it will certainly come, it will not delay long.
> —Habakkuk 2:2–3, NASB

Make yours concise, memorable, and portable.

Check out the Vision Engine (VSN NGN), an AI-powered interactive tool designed to help you clarify your vision, align your goals, and chart your next steps.

EXERCISE
Crafting Your Vision

Time to invest in yourself. Give yourself an hour uninterrupted to reflect and write. Don't worry about grammar or how it sounds. Suspend judgment and let your answers flow.

Who am I when no one is watching and no one is judging me?
_____
_____
_____

What values do I want my life to consistently reflect?
_____
_____
_____

When have I felt most like myself? What was I doing?
_____
_____
_____

What breaks my heart or makes me feel deeply moved?
_____
_____
_____

What kind of problems do I feel uniquely drawn to solve?
_____
_____
_____

If I had all the time and money I needed, what would I still choose to do?
_____
_____
_____

What activities make me feel energized?
_____
_____
_____

What legacy do I want to leave behind in the lives of others?
_____
_____
_____

Take a moment for a self-check. How are you feeling after this reflection? Are you inspired, anxious, hopeful, or maybe uncertain? Just notice what's coming up, and jot it down. Let your answers rise naturally, without judgment.

_____
_____
_____

The Results Tree

Who do I feel called to become?

_____
_____
_____

Begin to explore your vision across these major areas of life:

Faith and your spiritual journey

_____
_____
_____

Fulfillment and personal development

_____
_____
_____

Family and close relationships

_____
_____
_____

Fitness and physical well-being

_____
_____
_____

Finance and how you manage or grow resources

_____
_____
_____

Fun and recreational joy

_____
_____
_____

Future and long-term dreams

_____
_____
_____

Freedom and your sense of autonomy

_____
_____
_____

Friendship and meaningful connection

_____
_____
_____

Focus and clarity of mind

_____
_____
_____

Fidelity and commitment

_____
_____
_____

Fortitude and inner strength

_____
_____
_____

Next, identify your core values. What principles are nonnegotiable for you? Perhaps it's love, integrity, creativity, faith, adventure, or generosity. These values should guide the language and heart of your vision.

_____
_____
_____
_____
_____

Now picture yourself in the future, one year, three years, five years, ten years or more. Imagine living with intentionality and purpose. Continue writing: What does your life look like? Whom are you with? What impact are you making?

_____
_____
_____
_____

WRITE YOUR VISION

- » When you write your vision, use the present tense. Let it feel alive. For example: "I am a present and loving father, using my gifts to lead with authenticity and serve others through my calling."

- » Keep it grounded and real but also bold enough to stretch and inspire you. If it doesn't move you, it won't guide you. If it doesn't feel like yours, it won't stick.

- » Edit until it's clear and concise. Aim for two to four strong sentences that feel personal and motivating. Then, summarize it in a single line you can remember and live by.

- » Finally, test your vision against your daily decisions. A strong vision becomes your compass. Ask yourself regularly, "Does this align with my vision?" Let it guide your path, and don't be afraid to refine it as you grow.

Here are some sample visions for inspiration:

The Purposeful Leader

I grew up watching people work hard but feel unseen. I want my life to help others realize their voice, lead with integrity, and uplift their communities. My faith grounds me, but I walk with people from all walks of life. I lead to make change that lasts beyond me. **Vision statement:** I lead to uplift the overlooked and build leaders who serve with purpose.

The Rooted Family Builder

I want my home to be a steady place where love, faith, and good food are shared daily. We don't need fancy things, just time together, respect, and a roof that holds laughter. What I build with my hands is meant to support the people under my roof. **Vision statement:** I build a grounded, joyful home where my family thrives and blesses others.

The Creative Visionary

The world doesn't always have a place for people like me, so I make my own stage. My art challenges assumptions, reveals hidden beauty, and invites others to feel seen. I create because silence feels like dying, and expression is how I serve. **Vision statement:** I create to awaken, to heal, and to make space for inclusion.

The Healing Presence

People carry silent pain. I want to be a soft landing for those who feel alone, whether at a bedside, across a kitchen table, or in a passing moment. When I am centered in peace, I help others find their way back to themselves. **Vision statement:** I bring calm and healing to others through presence, compassion, and quiet strength.

The Disciplined Builder
I come from a place where opportunity was scarce, so I don't waste mine. I plan carefully, work steadily, and build systems that serve people, not just profits. Discipline gave me freedom, and now I teach others how to multiply that gift. **Vision statement:** I build scalable systems and success through discipline, vision, and generosity.

Your vision:

_____
_____
_____
_____
_____
_____

Before moving forward, pause and ask yourself, "If I'm not committed, what's holding me back? What do I need to overcome that resistance?"

"If I am committed to this journey, I'll take 100 percent responsibility."

Sign: _____

Date: _____

Chapter 3

Connecting Goals to Your Vision

Vision without action is merely a dream. Action without vision just passes the time. Vision with action can change the world.
Joel A. Barker

An ancient Greek proverb says, "A society grows when old men plant trees in whose shade they know they shall never sit." This statement illustrates a vision of impact far beyond our lifetimes, with the specific goal of planting trees for the good of the next generation, and perhaps the next and the next.

A clear vision is crucial. If your goals aren't absorbing strength and nutrients from your vision, you'll have a stunted tree, and maybe one that withers to nothing.

Jesus told a parable about a man who sowed seeds in four kinds of soil. Some fell on a hardened walkway, and the birds ate them. Others fell on a thin layer of dirt over rock. They sprouted but had shallow roots and didn't last in the heat of the sun. Others fell among weeds that choked out the growing plants, and finally, some fell on fertile soil and "produced a crop that was thirty, sixty, and even a hundred times as much as had been planted!" (Matthew 13:3–9, NLT). I want to apply the parable in this way: Your vision is your soil, and your goals are the seeds. All of us are planting seeds, but some of us aren't planting in the fertile soil of a compelling vision.

This is the primary point of this book. If you get this, you'll see every moment and every activity as an opportunity to fulfill your highest purpose in life. If you don't, you'll have scattered, disconnected goals. You'll fulfill some and neglect others, but even when you succeed in reaching some, they won't bring real fulfillment. Don't skip this step. Don't pass Go. Don't collect two hundred dollars. Stay here until you own this principle and it owns you.

First, it's important to define *goals* and *results*:

» A *goal* is "the object of a person's ambition or effort; an aim or desired result."
» A *result* is "a consequence, effect, or outcome of something."[28]

We often declare what we intend to do, what we believe our goals to be. The clearest indicator of our true intention is not what we say, how many times we write it down, or even how passionately we believe it. The clearest indicator is our results. Our outcomes are the evidence of our actual intentions, conscious or not.

For example, if I say I intend to invest three hundred dollars a month into a mutual fund but only contributed nine hundred over the course of a year, the result reveals that something else was at play. I may have had a conscious intention to invest consistently, but I likely had an unconscious intention that took priority, perhaps to soothe anxiety through spending, to avoid long-term commitments, or to stay in financial struggle to confirm a belief about myself.

> *"The good life is a process, not a state of being. It is a direction, not a destination."*
> CARL ROGERS, PSYCHOLOGIST

This is not about blame. It's about awareness. If we believe our lives are shaped by our intentions, and we see that our results don't align with what we said we wanted, it's a powerful moment to pause and ask: "What was my real intention? What belief or protection or pattern was I unknowingly serving?" Often the unconscious intention is rooted in fear, past wounding, or a need to stay consistent with a limiting belief.

It's a confronting and freeing realization. When we bring unconscious intention into the light, we gain the power to choose differently. Only then can our conscious goals become fully aligned with our actions and outcomes.

In the past I wasn't a big fan of feedback. I didn't want to hear anything but glowing compliments, and I was defensive and dismissive when I heard anything corrective. But as I've been using the principles of The Results Tree, I've come to the conclusion (a monumental one for me) that honest feedback is a form of love. People who have the courage to speak into my life and point out both what's working and what's not working—where I'm on track and where I'm off track—are demonstrating genuine love. They want the best for me, even if it makes the relationship uncomfortable for a moment. It would be easier for them to find excuses to avoid the conversation. They might assume what they've observed "isn't a big deal" or "he'll figure it out on his own." But they cared enough to wade in, tell me what they've seen, and encourage me to be a better leader, husband, father, and friend. I believe it's true, feedback is love.

Our current results in life are not just the product of our thinking; they're a reflection of our deepest affections. It's not simply what we believe or know that drives behavior but what our hearts are most drawn to. If my affections aren't captured and redirected by a compelling vision, I will continue setting goals I never fully pursue, or worse, I'll achieve them and still feel hollow. This is why lasting change isn't just about willpower or strategy; it's about the transformation of desire. Vision isn't just about where I'm going, it's about what I love most.

Professor J. K. A. Smith asserts that what we love is more powerful than our thoughts. "We are not static 'bobbleheads,' but dynamic actors constantly being pulled towards our loves. In this sense, we are, as human beings, primarily 'lovers.' And, as Augustine would argue, when those loves are oriented rightly, we will flourish as human beings, made in the image of God."[29] Certainly, some of us are more cerebral than others, but if you have a pulse, you have passion. Find it, name it, nurture it, and let it ground your vision and catalyze your results.

What were your goals over the past year? Think of key areas of your life, such as finances, fitness, and family. If a research analyst looked at your results, what would they conclude? If you didn't achieve what you thought were your goals, what do your results tell you?

Sometimes when we look back at our goals, it's tempting to judge ourselves by what we declared, what we said we wanted to do or achieve. The truth is that our results reveal something deeper than our words. Every outcome is evidence of the strongest intention at play, whether conscious or unconscious. If your results don't match what you said you wanted, it doesn't mean you failed; it means another, often hidden, intention was at work. That intention might have been shaped by fear, limiting beliefs, or protective patterns that live below the surface. The question then becomes not "Why didn't I reach my goal?" but "What intention was running in me that created this result?"

ORIGINS

Where do our goals come from? What's the origin? What has shaped them over the years? These aren't simple questions for most of us. Perhaps the most powerful influence was our home environment when we were kids. Some of us admired our father or mother and wanted to emulate what we saw in them. If our parents were diligent, we were determined to be diligent. If our parents were creative, we internalized the freedom to try new things. Children can also repeat negative behaviors rooted in their family atmosphere. If our parents were harsh and condemning, we may be very lenient with our kids. Kristie and I both had parents who would take us shoe shopping only at Payless ShoeSource through middle school. This was especially challenging with athletic shoes, as the store brand hurt our feet. As a result, Kristie and I both love buying Nikes for our kids today. Similarly, if our parents were absent in our lives, we may have made a heartfelt commitment to be kind to our children. Another factor is peer pressure. In our formative years in junior high and high school our group of friends had a direct impact on the trajectory of our lives, for better or worse. Some of us have been influenced by doors that have closed, sometimes unexpectedly and traumatically, so our goals shrank with our diminished outlook.

Let me ask, Why did you choose to move boldly toward a big goal or drift away in self-doubt? In what ways have you wanted to be like your parents, and in what ways have you done everything in your power to be the exact opposite? You may have had a boss or mentor who believed in you when you didn't believe in yourself, so your goals expanded to include new possibilities. Who has been the most positive influence in helping you reach for more?

"Setting goals is the first step in turning the invisible into the visible."
TONY ROBBINS

Understanding the origins of our goals helps us see them more objectively and determine whether they're rooted in a bigger vision. We may realize that to avoid failure, we set our sights too low, and a new sense of purpose can catapult us to reach for more. Or we may see that our goals have been misplaced. We may have had challenging goals and plenty of drive, but we were on a path that was not authentic.

START WITH YOUR VISION

For years I started my yearly, quarterly, monthly, and weekly planning by listing my goals because I was taught this is a good step toward being successful. A few years ago I realized I'd missed the larger purpose. When we start with a vision, the actual goals may stay the same, but they're now connected to a higher purpose. As a result, we have a deeper motivation and a higher likelihood of achieving them.

Whatever it takes, identify and clarify your vision. Yes, you'll adjust it as you gain more insights and experience. You're not coming up with something out of thin air. Your vision taps into passions already within you and waiting to be released. It has been waiting for you since the dawn of time.

For some folks their goals may have been adopted from someone else or from their culture or from social media. In some cases goals may be the product of pressure to perform from a parent or an authority figure. If you are a pleaser like me, it is motivating to get approval for setting big goals and again for achieving them. However, there is an emptiness and a weakness that come with setting or achieving goals that are not rooted in your vision.

Even when we feel we've been treated unfairly, we still get to take responsibility. We aren't responsible for what others did to us, but once we're adults, we are responsible for how we respond to what happened and decisions that follow. If we refuse to own our current life, we stay stuck and often have no idea why. This is especially true when we blame others and let bitterness or self-pity drain our joy, when we excuse people instead of being honest about the harm, or when we deny our hurt altogether.

I'm not saying you should feel good about traumatic experiences or pretend they didn't matter. We all need space to grieve and heal our wounds. But you also have a God-given opportunity and responsibility to shape your life now, in this moment, today. Hard times can crush us or cultivate something powerful within us; the difference is our perspective. A wise person once said that the pains we endure in the first half of life often become the foundation of our greatest impact in the second half. Pain can become fertile soil where wisdom, compassion, and strength take root and grow. Appendix

C will help you become more aware of how your past has formed you and how you can move forward with clarity and purpose.

A Framework for Goals

There are several proven goal-setting frameworks out there, and if you've found one that works for you, by all means stick with it. The real power isn't in the tool itself but in how consistently and intentionally you use it. However, if you're still looking for a structure that brings clarity, focus, and momentum, I recommend starting with SMART goals. This framework is simple, widely used, and highly effective, especially when you're building the discipline of taking meaningful, consistent action. Appendix B provides space to detail your SMART goals and then track each one. Let's take a closer look at how SMART goals can support your Results Tree journey and help you turn vision into the life you really want.

- » Specific: What will be accomplished?
- » Measurable: How will you measure success?
- » Achievable: Do you have the requisite resources and skills?
- » Relevant: Why is it important? And more pointedly for us, how does the goal align with your vision?
- » Time-bound: What is the due date for success?

One, Then the Other

Before you jump into a goal-setting posture, make sure you keep the vision for your life clearly in mind. Write it down on a sticky note and post it in front of your workspace. Look at it as you make decisions so it becomes part of your decision-making process. Your goals should be rooted directly in your vision. If they aren't, reconsider them, adjust them, or replace them. Obviously, this takes more time and attention than just going through the motions, but you picked up this book because you want something more profound. Do the work. It's worth it.

This is your "tombstone test," and it's a test you'll take every time you set a goal and make a decision to achieve it or not. Sooner or later the question will lodge deep in your soul: Will this goal, this choice, this action lead to the kind of obituary I want someone to read at my funeral? Or, to put it another way, will the pursuit of this goal fulfill my vision? (See appendix A to write the obituary you'd like people to read and hear at your funeral.)

Consider the wide range of possible goals. Some of life's most important domains can be captured by these eleven F's, a framework that has helped countless individuals align with their vision and generate epic results:

» Faith—spirituality and belief
» Fulfillment—personal growth
» Family—relationships with loved ones
» Fitness—physical health and well-being
» Finance—money management and wealth
» Fun—leisure, hobbies, and recreation
» Freedom—autonomy
» Friendships—social connections
» Focus—mental clarity and concentration

- » Fidelity—commitment and trust in relationships
- » Fortitude—resilience and inner strength

THE DOMAINS OF ACTION

For the exercise at the end of this chapter, pick your top three domains as your priorities. Mine are faith, family, and finance. To be honest, faith and family are harder to quantify than finances. One is inherently measurable; the others take more creativity to know you are on the right track. These three are more important to me than the others; in fact, they have a major impact on everything else. My heart and my most important relationships aren't transformed if my primary focus is on losing a few pounds. If a richer, deeper experience of the grace of God captures my heart, every other aspect of my life will be infused with love, wisdom, and compassion.

Use the worksheets at the end of this chapter to write your SMART goals for each of the three areas you choose, and at the top of each one, answer this question: "How will achieving this goal contribute to fulfilling my vision?" Don't make quick assumptions. Stay with this question for a while, wrestle with it, and make sure you're aligning your goals with your vision. Ask yourself: "Why this goal?" "Why now?" "What's so important about it?"

Then, examine the rest of the list, and pick one or two areas where positive change would have the biggest impact on your life. You might have $50,000 in credit card debt, a strained relationship with a family member, a chronic lack of sleep, broken trust with your colleagues, or something else that came to mind as soon as you read the list of domains. Focus on one or two additional domains to work on, state your clear intentions, and take committed action.

Stuck and discouraged people may feel overwhelmed by the idea of setting goals, some because they seem irrelevant and others because they're already so stressed or self-condemning that they never want to fail again. When they have a clear, compelling vision about making a difference, paralyzed people will be motivated, and discouraged people will have hope. Those who are successful but empty are probably pros at goal setting. They've met countless goals, met them on time, and achieved great success. They need to dive deep into their hearts to uncover a hidden passion. What injustice makes them angry? What hurts draw out their compassion?

If you just set out to be liked, you will be prepared to compromise on anything at any time and will achieve nothing.
MARGARET THATCHER

Some of us "live in our heads," disconnected from our hearts, but when we break through our fear of exposing our hearts and unlock our passion for a higher purpose, we'll experience incredible motivation. Through clear intention we will do whatever it takes to accomplish what we have set before ourselves. When we find this key to our hearts, we'll engage our talents and creativity for others, not just for ourselves. Then, setting goals will be connected to a consuming vision to make a difference. We'll have a powerful why.

Fulfillment is a tricky goal and often misunderstood. For some, it becomes a self-centered pursuit of knowledge, power, or prestige. For others, especially those who feel unworthy or insignificant, the idea of seeking fulfillment feels out of reach or even selfish. Once again, it comes back to vision. A compelling vision, one that seeks to heal your soul, love well, serve others, and uplift the world around you, can transform even the most self-serving pursuits into lives of meaning. If you're one of the many people who carry deep wounds or a sense of emptiness, experiencing God's grace and allowing it to fill the gaps in your heart is a worthy and life-changing aim. I've learned that you can't give what you don't have. If you want to impact your family, your colleagues, or your community in a lasting way, you must first allow your own heart to be filled with grace, love, and strength. When that happens, your ego will try to pull you off course, and you'll have the joy and discipline of choosing to return to the path. Again and again, this becomes the practice: staying rooted in grace connected to your source.

The Journey

Personal growth is always about the why—the purpose, vision, or dream—and the why becomes clearer with experience. Don't be frustrated if you discover that your current vision needs some refinement. That's just part of the process. Individuals, families, companies, and organizations need a clear sense of purpose. Simon Sinek explains, "We are drawn to leaders and organizations that are good at communicating what they believe. Their ability to make us feel like we belong, to make us feel special, safe and not alone is part of what gives them the ability to inspire us."[30] This applies just as well to spouses, parents, friends, and everyone else in our sphere of relationships. We can make them feel that they belong and that they're special. When people feel understood and loved, they're easy to inspire.

My journey is prioritized in this order: God, self, spouse, family, purpose, and business. That order matters. When we start with God, we anchor our lives in a source greater than ourselves, one that brings clarity, grace, and conviction. From there, we must steward our own health, mentally, emotionally, physically, and spiritually, so we can show up whole for others. Only then can we fully invest in our spouse and family, not from a place of neediness or obligation but from genuine overflow. Our purpose flows naturally from this alignment, allowing us to contribute meaningfully to the world. Finally, business becomes the outward expression of all that is ordered within. Without this prioritization it's easy to chase success at the expense of the things that make life truly rich. When the foundation is strong, everything else can rise with stability and strength.

All of us need to lean on the wisdom others can provide, but selecting the source of input can be tricky. It's easy to ask the wrong person for advice, but only a fool keeps asking the same person for directions when they've demonstrated they are lost. In our family we advise that eagles shouldn't take flight plans from chickens.

Today, we have more advisers than at any time in history. Every influencer claims to be an expert, and in our polarized culture, humility is a vanishing trait. Everyone insists they're right. At the end of his most famous sermon, Jesus paints two pictures about the necessity of filtering input, and the consequences of our decisions to follow advice. First, He uses a metaphor for two kinds of trees:

> Beware of false prophets who come disguised as harmless sheep but are really vicious wolves. You can identify them by their fruit, that is, by the way they act. Can you pick grapes from thornbushes, or figs from thistles? A good tree produces good fruit, and a bad tree produces bad fruit. A good tree can't produce bad fruit, and a bad tree can't produce good fruit. So every tree that does not produce good

> fruit is chopped down and thrown into the fire. Yes, just as you can identify a tree by its fruit, so you can identify people by their actions.
> —Matthew 7:15–20, NLT

So don't rush to trust people. Do your homework. Be patient and look for the fruit in an adviser's life, not just of glamor, riches, and fame, but of integrity, wisdom, and humility. You will become like the people you trust. That's a warning and a promise.

The second picture is of two builders. This time Jesus is inviting His listeners (and us, as readers) to pay attention to the site where we construct our lives. As we've seen, most people build on a foundation of popularity, possessions, prestige, and power. These promise stability, but they eventually (and inevitably) fail, resulting in shame, confusion, and losses of many kinds. There's only one sure bedrock on which we should build. Jesus concluded His message:

> Anyone who listens to my teaching and follows it is wise, like a person who builds a house on solid rock. Though the rain comes in torrents and the floodwaters rise and the winds beat against that house, it won't collapse because it is built on bedrock. But anyone who hears my teaching and doesn't obey it is foolish, like a person who builds a house on sand. When the rains and floods come and the winds beat against that house, it will collapse with a mighty crash.
> —Matthew 7:24–27, NLT

Don't wait for a "mighty crash" to inspect your foundation. Do it now. Some people learn from their own disasters, others learn by watching others crash, and a few learn by hearing truths and acting on them. If you've created your own disaster, make God's love and strength your new foundation. If you've watched others make a mess of their lives and decided to build your life on Jesus the Rock, good for you! If you've read the Scriptures and consistently tailored your agenda to fit God's, you're a rare breed. No matter which of these people you are, it's never too late to move to or rebuild your house on the right foundation.

You don't have to go on this journey alone. In fact, you *shouldn't* go alone. We are relational creatures; even the most introverted among us need strong relationships (just fewer of them). If you are sinking into a quagmire of debt, find a financial counselor to help you make better choices and chart a course to financial freedom. If you struggle with past hurts messing up present relationships, find a counselor who can help you choose healing. If you want to be a better spouse, parent, or leader, find a mentor who has a track record of effectively helping others. No matter what, find a friend or two who listens more than they talk, who invites you to be honest and doesn't run away or laugh when you open your heart. You need someone who doesn't depend on you for his or her career. In other words, don't pick someone who has a built-in incentive to tell you what you want to hear. All of us need honest, wise partners on the path.

I've served under some leaders who looked beyond and beneath some of my failures to see that I was doing my best with the information I had at the time. Sometimes they stepped in to fix a mess I'd created, and it seemed easy for them because they had more training, a lot more experience, and a better understanding of what was involved. One of the most memorable of my screwups was when I served as the director of tactics at the Combined Air Operations Center (CAOC) in Qatar. By sending an email, I inadvertently got a one-star general to supersede the authority of a three-star general. This seldom bodes well for the one-star and his staff! I was trying to do the right thing, but I put the one-star in a predicament. The next morning, the senior colonel told me to rescind the order I'd issued the previous night. I wrote a long, detailed email to explain the change. When I showed it to the colonel before I sent it, he said, "Don't explain. Don't defend. Just rescind the order." With major deletions, the email I sent read: "The order sent last night at 23:37 hours on the use of tactic X is hereby rescinded." I learned two lessons that day: Pause and think twice before you send an impactful email to be sure you don't make a dumb mistake, and when you do make a mistake, own it with responsibility and brevity; no one needs to hear your excuse. My mistake involved officers who outranked me. I took some ribbing for a few days. It was a mistake I didn't make again.

My commanding officer, like all good officers, knew that my mistake presented an opportunity for me to learn and grow. I had looked at the situation, examined the facts, and made what appeared to be the best decision at the moment, but I was wrong. For him this wasn't a fatal flaw, and he didn't treat the event as a catastrophe. He used it as a classroom for me to gain wisdom and experience.

When I took my first command, I encouraged my airmen to go out and break things. Be bold, take risks, and scare yourself from time to time. Growth can only happen outside your comfort zone. Failure is never the end of the world unless you believe it is. Some of the most productive people in history have been willing to attempt what they'd never tried before, simply to see what might happen. If it succeeds, celebrate. If it fails, learn. With every success, ask what worked—with every failure, don't bury it; study it. Be curious enough to look failure in the eye and ask, "What can I learn from this?" When you fail, fail forward. Keep injecting energy into yourself and your leadership, and encourage those around you to be bold too. The inscription inside my academy class ring still inspires me: "The only failure is failure not to try."

Kristie's journey echoes this truth from another angle. She learned to see results as neutral, neither inherently good nor bad but always instructive. After working in the fast-paced world of MGM Studios, she pivoted into real estate to carry on the family business. She invested time and energy, but once licensed, she knew it wasn't her path. Walking away wasn't failure; it was wisdom. When her father passed away, she realized life was short and returned to her core passions of philanthropy, public speaking, and politics. By realigning with her purpose, Kristie found greater peace and fulfillment. Each day now feels empowered and aligned with the vision God has given her, me, and our family.

Together we've learned that there is no magic button to make life fall into place. The journey itself is the success. Each step, forward, sideways, or even backward, is worth celebrating. Missteps teach as much as victories, and both refine us for what's ahead. The daily question isn't, "Did I avoid failure?" but rather, "Did I stay on the path toward my vision? Did I bring meaning into my day? Did I make a difference in someone's life?" When the answer is yes, results, whatever they look like, become milestones of growth, not measures of worth.

Those who expect a quick fix invariably become discouraged and quit. Those who understand that the process is as important as (and maybe more important than) the outcome will stick with it. And the benefits are truly life-changing! Isn't that what you want in life? A study of six thousand people conducted by Patrick Hill, an assistant professor of psychology at Carleton University, found that "people with a sense of purpose had a 15 percent lower risk of death, compared with those who said they were more or less aimless. And it didn't seem to matter when people found their direction. It could be in their 20s, 50s or 70s." The study controlled other factors that affect longevity: age, gender, emotional well-being, and others. "A sense of purpose trumped all that." Hill asserts that purpose provides a "compass or lighthouse that provides an overarching aim and direction in day-to-day lives." The article about the study concludes, "Purposeful individuals may simply lead healthier lives ... but it also could be that a sense of purpose protects against the harmful effects of stress."

The failure to identify and clarify our purpose, then, increases stress and can have significantly detrimental effects on our health. Unrelieved stress produces a wide range of problems: physical problems, including headaches and muscle tension; social problems, such as strained relationships; and psychological problems, such as anxiety and depression. We can't avoid all stress, but having a sense of purpose relieves at least some of the effects of stress and helps us cope more effectively with the rest. The study points to an important conclusion: Not having a sense of purpose can ruin your health and contribute to an early death.[31]

CHECKPOINTS

Don Miguel Ruiz wrote a powerful book called *The Four Agreements*. In just a few pages he offers deep wisdom that gently reveals the self-limiting beliefs and unconscious patterns that keep us stuck. His four simple agreements aren't rules; they're invitations. When we live by them, they open the door to greater freedom, joy, and love. I've taken them to heart and made them part of my daily self-check. They help me return to center and stay aligned with my vision.

1. **Be impeccable with your word.** Speak truthfully, clearly, and with kindness. No lies, no blame, no manipulation.
2. **Don't take anything personally.** What others say or do is about them, not you. Let go of the need to defend or react.
3. **Don't make assumptions.** Ask, clarify, and listen. Don't fill in blanks with fiction or fear.
4. **Always do your best.** Show up fully. Give what you have, with intention, not excuses.[32]

These four agreements are simple yet incredibly profound and practical!

Here's a very specific and concrete example: A few days before I wrote this chapter, my teenage son Preston told me he wanted to attend an event with some friends. I said, "Cool. Be sure to take your phone so you can contact us if you need to."

He looked at his phone and said, "It's dead. I don't need it anyway." He started to walk out the door.

I replied, "No, I want you to take your phone, so you need to charge it before you go." I then told him, "I'm going for a walk. I'll be back later. Charge your phone."

"I'll be late," he insisted.

"Too bad," was my impatient reply.

Preston wasn't impressed with my parenting skills at that moment. On my walk I thought about our interaction, and I realized I hadn't treated him with kindness and respect. I could have said, "Son, your phone will charge in just a few minutes, and then you can go. Your friends won't mind waiting that long. Have fun!" But that's not what I said, and my face and tone of voice weren't patient and supportive. When I walked back into the house,

I apologized to Preston for my reaction to the situation, and I explained what I should have done. "I'll try to do better next time," I promised.

I had violated all of the four agreements: I had been harsh instead of being impeccable with my words; I had taken Preston's resistance personally and barked at him; I had made an assumption that he couldn't figure things out on his own, so I'd given a command instead of inviting him into the process; and I certainly hadn't done my best in that moment. It was a good learning experience for me and, I trust, for my son. If I hadn't intuitively known my response was out of alignment with my vision, I might have continued down a dark path of grumbling about Preston being so irresponsible, and he might have built up some resentment that would show up in our next interaction and many more until it was resolved.

My moment with Preston was small, but the lesson was lasting. It reminded me how ordinary interactions can reveal the gap between who I want to be and how I actually show up. For most of us, these moments feel manageable, but others might think, "Sure, that's easy for you, but you don't know what I've been through." I understand. Life can be brutal, and your story matters. Yet the moment we say, "Yeah, but...," we step through a chicken exit. It becomes the escape hatch that keeps us trapped as victims of circumstance instead of authors of our next chapter.

The truth is that every one of us has the ability to overcome our past and write a new future, no matter how painful the story has been. Our past may explain how we got here, but it doesn't have to define who we become. Many have endured unimaginable suffering, and through their response, they've shown what it means to live from a vision greater than themselves. Few embodied this truth more powerfully than Viktor Frankl. If anyone ever had the right to give up or to let suffering dictate his outlook, it was

Frankl. His life reminds us that while we cannot always choose our circumstances, we can always choose our response.

Another great illustration of these four agreements is the story of Frankl, an Austrian psychiatrist who disagreed with the nihilism of the 1930s in Europe and believed every person's life has meaning. His beliefs were tested when the Nazis took over his country and made life unbearable for Jews. He had an opportunity to escape with his pregnant wife, Tilly, but he didn't want to leave his parents to face Hitler's thugs alone. His father showed him marble carvings from a synagogue that had been destroyed by the Germans, and one of them was the Ten Commandments. It read, "Honor thy father and mother." In that moment, he decided that he and his wife would stay with his parents and face the unknown future together. It was a bleak future. His father died in Terezin Ghetto, his mother and brother perished at Auschwitz, and his wife died at Bergen-Belsen. During his imprisonment in four different concentration camps, he reached out to help other prisoners cope with isolation, the constant stench of death, and rampant hopelessness. Frankl's commitment to finding meaning in every circumstance led him to the conclusion, "When we are no longer able to change a situation, we are challenged to change ourselves." After liberation in 1945 he wrote a manuscript that was eventually titled *Man's Search for Meaning*. It was an international best seller and is still recommended as one of Amazon's Top 100 Books to Read in a Lifetime. His perspective is summed up in this statement: "The one thing you can't take away from me is the way I choose to respond to what you do to me. The last of one's freedoms is to choose one's attitude in any given circumstance. Happiness cannot be pursued; it must ensue. Life is never made unbearable by circumstances, but only by lack of meaning and purpose."[33] Please make it a point to read his book.

Some people are successful but unfulfilled. By all accounts my friend Brad was a success. He had risen in the insurance sales business from the early years of cold calls and persuading family members to having his own agency with several employees and a solid book of business. He was making plenty of money, but he felt that something was missing. For years he had been interested in financial planning, but it always seemed out of reach. When he was about fifty years old, he took a long, hard look at his life, evaluated his finances, talked to his wife many times, and decided to take the plunge. After making the choice to change careers, he told a friend, "A lot of people think I'm crazy to give up such a profitable business, but I believe this is what I was made to do. I'm all in." For the next couple of years, Brad took classes, studied, and passed his exams. Then, he had to start from scratch to find clients, just as he had decades before in the insurance business. It took three years to build up his business, but he didn't mind the struggle. He was convinced his purpose was to help people with their money. His clients were mostly people of means, and Brad also wanted to help young people get started. He launched a podcast for college students and recent graduates, and soon a local university asked him to teach a class every semester on the basics of financial management. Brad paid a price to pursue his vision, but the smile on his face and the energy he brings to every conversation say loudly and clearly, "It's worth it! I'm on purpose!"

Thankfully, most of us will never endure the horrors Frankl faced, and his story reminds us that purpose isn't born in comfort. Meaning is forged in adversity, in the moments when we choose strength rather than collapse. The same truth applies to each of us. Whether it's clarifying your vision, learning through relationships, or finding grace after failure, growth always begins with acknowledging the situation for what it is and taking responsibility for your response.

My own failures have become some of my greatest teachers. They've taught me patience, humility, and compassion, the kind you can't fake. I've also learned that the more I share those lessons, the more I grow. Transformation isn't a single event; it's a daily practice. Every decision to try again, to get back in the arena, every moment of humility, every act of grace is a quiet declaration that our stories aren't over.

That's how pain becomes purpose. That's how we move from surviving to serving. And that's how I've chosen to pay it forward.

EXERCISES

Now that you've read Viktor Frankl's story, where in your own life are you still allowing a victim narrative to shape your choices, your attitude, or your vision?

_____
_____
_____

What would it look like to reclaim that power and respond instead with purpose?

_____
_____
_____

What were your goals over the past year?

_____
_____
_____

What was your motivation to achieve them?

_____
_____
_____

How well did each one work out? What are the actual results?

_____
_____
_____

What does it mean to connect your goals to your vision, your sense of purpose?

_____
_____
_____
_____

What difference does that (or would that) make for you?

_____
_____
_____
_____

Explain how having a sense of meaning and purpose gave Viktor Frankl the heart and will to keep looking up during his time in the concentration camp while his family members were murdered.

_____
_____
_____
_____

Can you relate at all to Brad's story? If so, what are the connections?

_____
_____
_____
_____

Analyzing Your Goals

Write the vision statement you created in the previous chapter here so it stays fresh in your mind:

_____
_____
_____
_____
_____
_____
_____

List your top three domains from the list on page 67:

1. _____
2. _____
3. _____

FIRST-DOMAIN SMART GOAL

Identify a goal you most want to pursue in your first domain. Write this goal below, and then complete the questions on the **SMART Goal Worksheet** on the following pages regarding this goal.

_____
_____
_____
_____
_____

SMART GOAL WORKSHEET

S SPECIFIC	What will be accomplished?
M MEASURABLE	How will you measure success?
A ACHIEVABLE	Do you have the requisite resources and skills?
R RELEVANT	Why is it important? How does the goal align with your vision?
T TIME-BOUND	What is the due date for success?

TRACK YOUR GOAL

On the **SMART Goal Tracker** below, record your plan for achieving the goal you analyzed on the **SMART Goal Worksheet** on the previous page.

SMART GOAL TRACKER

	Date/Time of Goal	Measurable: How will I measure success?	Achievable: My plan on how to achieve the goal, notes on my progress, and revelations from my efforts
WEEK 1			
WEEK 2			
WEEK 3			

	Date/Time of Goal	Measurable: How will I measure success?	Achievable: My plan on how to achieve the goal, notes on my progress, and revelations from my efforts
WEEK 4			
WEEK 5			
WEEK 6			
WEEK 7			
WEEK 8			

	Date/Time of Goal	Measurable: How will I measure success?	Achievable: My plan on how to achieve the goal, notes on my progress, and revelations from my efforts
WEEK 9			
WEEK 10			
WEEK 11			
WEEK 12			
WEEK 13			

After you complete all thirteen weeks, reflect back on what worked and what didn't work.

___

SECOND-DOMAIN SMART GOAL

Identify a goal you most want to pursue in your second domain. Write this goal below, and then complete the questions on the **SMART Goal Worksheet** on the following pages regarding this goal.

___

SMART GOAL WORKSHEET

S SPECIFIC	What will be accomplished?
M MEASURABLE	How will you measure success?
A ACHIEVABLE	Do you have the requisite resources and skills?
R RELEVANT	Why is it important? How does the goal align with your vision?
T TIME-BOUND	What is the due date for success?

TRACK YOUR GOAL

On the **SMART Goal Tracker** below, record your plan for achieving the goal you analyzed on the **SMART Goal Worksheet** on the previous page.

SMART GOAL TRACKER

	Date/Time of Goal	Measurable: How will I measure success?	Achievable: My plan on how to achieve the goal, notes on my progress, and revelations from my efforts
WEEK 1			
WEEK 2			
WEEK 3			

	Date/Time of Goal	Measurable: How will I measure success?	Achievable: My plan on how to achieve the goal, notes on my progress, and revelations from my efforts
WEEK 4			
WEEK 5			
WEEK 6			
WEEK 7			
WEEK 8			

Connecting Goals to Your Vision 93

	Date/Time of Goal	Measurable: How will I measure success?	Achievable: My plan on how to achieve the goal, notes on my progress, and revelations from my efforts
WEEK 9			
WEEK 10			
WEEK 11			
WEEK 12			
WEEK 13			

After you complete all thirteen weeks, reflect back on what worked and what didn't work.

_____
_____
_____
_____
_____
_____
_____
_____
_____
_____

THIRD-DOMAIN SMART GOAL

Identify a goal you most want to pursue in your third domain. Write this goal below, and then complete the questions on the **SMART Goal Worksheet** on the following pages regarding this goal.

_____
_____
_____
_____
_____
_____

SMART GOAL WORKSHEET

S SPECIFIC	What will be accomplished?
M MEASURABLE	How will you measure success?
A ACHIEVABLE	Do you have the requisite resources and skills?
R RELEVANT	Why is it important? How does the goal align with your vision?
T TIME-BOUND	What is the due date for success?

TRACK YOUR GOAL

On the **SMART Goal Tracker** below, record your plan for achieving the goal you analyzed on the **SMART Goal Worksheet** on the previous page.

SMART GOAL TRACKER

	Date/Time of Goal	Measurable: How will I measure success?	Achievable: My plan on how to achieve the goal, notes on my progress, and revelations from my efforts
WEEK 1			
WEEK 2			
WEEK 3			

Connecting Goals to Your Vision 97

	Date/Time of Goal	Measurable: How will I measure success?	Achievable: My plan on how to achieve the goal, notes on my progress, and revelations from my efforts
WEEK 4			
WEEK 5			
WEEK 6			
WEEK 7			
WEEK 8			

The Results Tree

	Date/Time of Goal	Measurable: How will I measure success?	Achievable: My plan on how to achieve the goal, notes on my progress, and revelations from my efforts
WEEK 9			
WEEK 10			
WEEK 11			
WEEK 12			
WEEK 13			

After you complete all thirteen weeks, reflect back on what worked and what didn't work.

_____
_____
_____
_____
_____
_____
_____
_____
_____
_____
_____
_____

Chapter 4

CLEAR INTENTIONS
Goals That Really Matter

*We can either make our choices deliberately or allow
other people's agendas to control our lives.*
GREG MCKEOWN

When you declare your carefully crafted goals, you step into the light of responsibility and accountability with focus and clear intention. You may not have results yet, but you believe, without proof, they are coming. You are energized by possibility. You are committed to no more hedging, no more vagueness, no more self-deception. You have done the work, have built SMART goals, and are nearly ready to launch. One critical step remains. You must be committed to being deeply honest with yourself along this journey, and boldly, with crystal-clear intention, declare your goals that are grounded in your vision and pointed toward the life you really want.

This step is more important than many realize. When we hesitate and say things such as, "I think I might want to," or qualify our goals with conditions such as, "only if everything lines up," or, "I hope," we

CLEAR INTENTIONS

are looking for a way out. Kristie and I call this the chicken exit, taken from the signs on the walls of amusement parks where folks can exit the ride early if they don't like the way things are going. When we leave a chicken exit, it will be used when things get hard, and they will get hard, because right now your ego is terrified you may actually change this time. One vague, unmet goal makes it easier to abandon the next, and soon we return to business as usual, generating excuses rather than results. Any lack of clarity and commitment allows us to be pulled back into the gravity of old habits. This negative muscle memory has kept us and will continue to keep us stuck in mediocrity if we give it the slightest breath of air. Be vigilant, aware, present, and honest, and if you waver, phone a friend, ask for help, and be vulnerable. This is why declaring our goals to our most trusted allies is critical, so when we waver, they know what we are committed to and can support us through the tough patch until we get our mojo back.

Toughing it and going it alone reshackles us to the chain that holds us in self-deception. Just as people lie to others through exaggeration or omission, we lie to ourselves in subtle, crafty ways. If we are not committed to our vision with clear intention to achieve our goals, we might tell ourselves it doesn't really matter, that no one is being hurt, or that the problem is already solved. Sometimes we pretend that articulating goals is unnecessary, that it's better to just feel our way through things. Other times we convince ourselves we are not capable and give up before we begin. Those of us who are true masters of self-deception believe that fooling ourselves is something other people struggle with, not us.

We deceive ourselves for two main reasons. One is to reduce the stress of facing the possibility of future failure. The other is to feel important and competent in front of others. One helps us escape pain; the other seeks counterfeit approval without putting in the effort. Either way, self-deception will quietly derail a life or a career. The longer we do it, the more believable the lie becomes, until we mistake it for truth.

You may remember, Elizabeth Holmes was a biotech engineer who was at one time the darling of Wall Street. She hoodwinked investors, and now she's serving twenty years for fraud. Ken Lay and his partners at Enron developed an elaborate scheme to swindle stockholders, who filed a forty-billion-dollar lawsuit and ended up settling for about a sixth of that. Enron's bankruptcy was the largest in history at the time. Author David Robson explains:

> Our brains can fool us into believing things that are not true. Self-deception allows us to inflate our opinion of our own abilities, so that we believe we are smarter than everyone around us. It means that we overlook the repercussions of our actions for other people, so that we believe that we are generally acting in a moral way. And by deceiving ourselves about the veracity of our beliefs, we show greater conviction in our opinions—which can, in turn, help us to persuade others.... Tellingly, a desire for social status seems to increase people's tendency for self-deception.[34]

What can shake us out of the fog of self-delusion? Few people "just snap out of it" on their own. Most of the time we need an outside force to hold up a mirror so we can see the truth. Massive failure, being fired, confrontation with someone who sees through us, and near-death experiences can wake us up. Alcoholics and addicts often need to go to rehab after they "have a moment of clarity." Some of the rest of us need to rehab our hearts so we don't feel the need to deceive ourselves or others. To break free of the gravity of self-deception, our underlying beliefs need to be regularly challenged. Beliefs create thoughts, thoughts create feelings, feelings influence the actions we take, and our actions create our results, which always end up validating our beliefs. This is a self-reinforcing loop.

"People with clear, written goals, accomplish far more in a shorter period of time than people without them could ever imagine."

BRIAN TRACY

What's the way out? We can start by asking ourselves, "Is this really my vision? Are these goals consistent with my vision? What's getting in the way? Am I self-sabotaging?" And if we're wise, we'll find someone, a spouse, counselor, best friend, or mentor, who steps in to ask us penetrating questions. Whatever it takes, we need to find a way not to settle for excuses and lies. Many of us have lived our entire lives in a self-reinforcing loop, and now, with The Results Tree, we are stepping into our power and choosing a new story, choosing to create a new loop, a virtuous loop that will lead to a new and purposeful life. Expect to be challenged every step of the way.

And let's get real. Not every friend is a partner on the journey. I may be committed to losing twenty pounds in six months, but if my workout buddy says, "Hey, let's go get some ice cream when we leave the gym," he's more of an enabler than a partner. This is assuming, of course, that I've informed him of my goals. If I've kept it hidden or failed to set a clear intention, his offer is just a way to hang out together. We don't need to announce our goals to everyone, but those close to us need to know so they can encourage us to keep moving forward and avoid falling into old habit patterns.

THE FUEL

For me faith, fulfillment, and family fuel my progress. My vision is "I live grounded in faith, creating epic experiences." Being grounded in faith, I choose to create exciting, fulfilling experiences for myself, my family, and others around me. Daily I encounter countless distractions, both internally and externally, seeking to pull me off center, away from God's guidance and purpose.

Many of us can get caught up in the comparison and competition game, keeping up with the Joneses. If you have a fast car, I need one a little faster. If you buy a new house, I need to upgrade. If you went to the Rockies on vacation, I'm taking my family to the Alps. Our culture bombards us with so many shiny, pretty, glossy possessions and experiences that we're conditioned to believe we can't live without. These days, for every product we can find countless styles all across the price range. If you're like me, you'll be constantly tempted to buy the one just above what you can afford. That's not a big deal if we do it only occasionally with conscious intention, but often we do it over and over with each purchase. Take watches, for example. I love watches. You can buy a Casio at Walmart for $17.99, a Seiko for $119, a TAG Heuer for just over $2,000, a Rolex Submariner for $21,000, or a Patek Philippe Aquanaut for the "low, low" price of $105,000. You can get ground beef at your local supermarket, opt for a choice steak, upgrade to prime, or go all the way to Wagyu. And then there are smartphones, from basic to those with every conceivable feature. You get the idea. Before long we've maxed out our credit cards and sweat the due date every month, all because we value impressing people or making ourselves feel important more than we value freedom or inner peace. Pastor Rick Warren doesn't mince words: "It is foolish to buy things you don't need, with money you don't have, to impress people you don't like."[35]

"Efficiency is doing things right; effectiveness is doing the right things."
PETER DRUCKER

Clear intentions are the fuel that drives our commitment to disconnect from the cultural noise around us and reconnect with our identity, our calling, and our vision. When we do this, we create the space to shape a new reality, one where we can declare our goals without being drowned out or overwhelmed to always have more and better and different.

When we clearly communicate our vision and goals to others, our vision and goals become declarations, and declarations are powerful. They do not create reality by themselves, but they can set the direction and define the path toward a better future. That said, it is not enough to make a single declaration and hope for results. We need to keep our vision, our intentions, and our goals in front of us every day.

Write your goals where you will see them. Use a dry-erase marker on your bathroom mirror to remind yourself of them each morning. Add them to the top of your weekly to-do list. Some people may even choose to get them tattooed on as a symbol of total commitment. That kind of focus, that kind of visibility, changes how we live.

If we keep our vision and our goals constantly in front of us, sooner or later our dreams become deeply ingrained. They shift from conscious effort to a new operating system, and that is where the magic happens. When our goals and mindset become our default way of thinking and living, we begin to tap into the power of the unconscious mind. That is exactly what has happened to me.

Over time my vision has been refined and clarified, and that clarity has freed me to pursue bigger, bolder goals. I know my audacity intimidates some people, but it also inspires others. Kristie and I have big dreams for our family, and Kevin, my best friend and business partner, and I have set audacious goals for our company. Declaring our intentions has had a snowball effect. Each success builds momentum. Our goals grow, and so does our belief that we can achieve them. This is the power of a virtuous cycle, and it is working in our favor.

As Dan Sullivan and Dr. Benjamin Hardy explain in *10x Is Easier Than 2x*, "It's often easier to 10x your goals than to 2x them, because 10x forces you to rethink everything, while 2x tempts you to just work harder." That quote sums it up perfectly. Big vision changes everything.[36]

At our company, Excel Medical Staffing, we have always been committed to doing the small things well and trusting God to open doors, and that is exactly what has happened. The doors just didn't open the way I had planned on them. For years we worked exceptionally hard, always feeling as if success was just around the next bend. We pressed on in faith, continuing to invest time and money into the company.

Through reflection I came to a hard truth. I realized I was running the company for selfish reasons. I had seen others create massive wealth and recognition, and if I'm honest, that is what I was chasing. My goals for the company were out of alignment with my personal vision for my life. I was grounded in a belief that with more hard work I could force a win. As a result, I was not creating epic experiences for our team.

In the still of the night I made a commitment to refocus on people. Kevin and I overhauled our compensation plan, secured health-care benefits for our team, and made intentional efforts to pour energy into our people. We also introduced The Four Agreements as a foundational part of our culture. As these changes took root, everything shifted.

Around that time, a classmate of mine and Kevin's from the academy had been reaching out for months. He wanted advice on staffing for a decentralized clinical trial he was running. I was glad to help, offering insights along the way, often with the caveat, "I think you've got the wrong partner." For a while, nothing came of those conversations. Then, one day in February, the phone rang.

I picked up and, through a strong East Coast accent, heard: "Peak tells me you can solve my problem, and I think he's full of [bleep]." I laughed and said, "Well, hello."

That call changed everything.

My friend's company was struggling to get medical professionals to complete their clinical trial. That happens to be exactly what we do, so we mobilized on the spot. Our team worked through the weekend, determined to prove we could deliver precisely the type of professionals they needed. Those ninety-six hours became a defining moment in our company's story.

They must have liked what they saw, because they awarded us the largest contract we had ever received. Here's the truth: It didn't happen because we overpromised or tried to dazzle them. It happened because we had already declared our intention to invest in people and to serve with integrity and excellence. Refocusing on that commitment was a risk, but staying on the same path would have been an even greater one.

When it comes to risk, I have seen three kinds of people. Some avoid it altogether because they fear that failure will define them, and they become paralyzed. Others rush into risks recklessly because they feel pressure—financial, emotional, or imagined—and they are scrambling to catch up with where they think they *should* be.

Then there is a third group. These are the people who combine boldness with wisdom. They know not everything will work out, and they are OK with that. Though they know there are no guarantees, they still show up, fully invested, giving their best effort. My friend Jeff shared that most people overestimate risk and underestimate opportunity. That is why we cannot let fear keep us out of the arena, not if we want to live fully, lead boldly, and create lasting impact.

Our future is rooted in our self-perception. If we see ourselves as loved and secure, we'll have the freedom to dream big dreams. Our first declarations, then, are about ourselves. First (you saw this coming, didn't you?), we'll look at identity statements many of us repeat every day, consciously or subconsciously:

- "I've made too many mistakes to be forgiven."
- "My faith isn't strong enough to matter."
- "I'm too old, too far behind, or too broken to change."
- "People like me don't get to live out their dreams."
- "I'm the reason my family struggles."
- "If they really knew me, they wouldn't love me."
- "Why try? Nothing ever sticks for me."
- "I'm just not good with money."
- "People like me don't get rich; we survive."
- "I don't have time to enjoy life."
- "This is just the way life is. I don't have a choice."
- "People always leave, so why let them in?"
- "I can't trust myself to stay on task."
- "I can't be fully honest. No one would stick around."
- "I've failed too many times to bounce back now."

Do any of these sound familiar? Probably. But don't condemn yourself. These thoughts may have come from someone else or from past experiences. Whatever their origin, your subconscious will gladly hold on to them, not because they are true but because they create a sense of safety by keeping you small. That is the trick of the ego.

By now I'm sure you can see that these kinds of beliefs will not serve you moving forward. If you are committed to a big vision, it's going to require a new internal narrative. The voice between your ears needs an overhaul.

This is where affirmations come in. From the psalms to the Stoics to the mantras of Eastern traditions, people have long understood the power of spoken truth to reshape the mind and strengthen the heart. Words carry weight; repeated often enough, they plant seeds that grow into belief, and belief drives action.

So let's start with some replacements. Here are a few affirming statements we might begin telling ourselves:

- "I am worthy of love, success, and joy, just as I am!"
- "I am valuable and loved."
- "My past does not define me; it has prepared me."
- "I am fully equipped to handle the challenges in front of me."
- "I choose progress over perfection."
- "I speak truth to myself with kindness and clarity."
- "I am allowed to grow, change, and become more of who I was created to be."
- "I trust that God is guiding my steps and opening the right doors."
- "I create meaningful impact by showing up with purpose and integrity."
- "I don't chase approval; I walk in alignment with my values."
- "I make bold decisions with wisdom and faith."
- "I have everything I need to take the next step."
- "I am no longer afraid to be seen, heard, or challenged."
- "I release fear and embrace the opportunity in front of me."
- "I honor my vision by taking small, consistent steps every day."

Or, if you are a Christian, consider these affirmations, which aren't based on who *you think* you are but who *God says* you are:

- » "I am deeply and unconditionally loved by God." (See John 3:16.)
- » "He calls me His masterpiece, His treasure, created with purpose and care." (See Eph. 2:10.)
- » "Every sin I've ever committed, or will commit, has been fully forgiven through Christ." (See 1 John 1:9.)
- » "He delights in knowing me, not just from a distance but in every detail." (See Ps. 18:19; 139:1–4.)
- » "He sees all of me and still chooses to stay close." (See Ps. 145:18; Deut. 31:8.)
- » "His presence is with me always, in joy, in sorrow, and in silence." (See Matt. 28:20.)
- » "My life carries meaning because He gave it purpose." (See Jer. 29:11.)
- » "I don't have to earn love or worth. I already have them in Him." (See Rom. 8:38–39; Jer. 31:3.)
- » "In my weakness His strength shows up perfectly." (See 2 Cor. 12:9.)
- » "I am becoming who He designed me to be, one step at a time." (See Rom. 12:2; 8:29.)
- » "I have been adopted into His family, fully accepted and eternally secure." (See Eph. 1:5.)
- » "Jesus calls me His friend, and He walks with me in love and loyalty." (See John 15:15.)

The Bible is full of wonderful declarations about us. Let me point to three:

1. In Paul's letter to the Ephesians, after the introduction, he begins:

> Even before he made the world, God loved us and chose us in Christ to be holy and without fault in his eyes. God decided in advance to adopt us into his own family by bringing us to himself through Jesus Christ. This is what he wanted to do, and it gave him great pleasure. So we praise God for the glorious grace he has poured out on us who belong to his dear Son. He is so rich in kindness and grace that he purchased our freedom with the blood of his Son and forgave our sins. He has showered his kindness on us, along with all wisdom and understanding.
> —EPHESIANS 1:4–8, NLT

2. Later in the same letter Paul assures us:

> But God is so rich in mercy, and he loved us so much, that even though we were dead because of our sins, he gave us life when he raised Christ from the dead. (It is only by God's grace that you have been saved!) For he raised us from the dead along with Christ and seated us with him in the heavenly realms because we are united with Christ Jesus. So God can point to us in all future ages as examples of the incredible wealth of his grace and kindness toward us, as shown in all he has done for us who are united with Christ Jesus.
>
> God saved you by his grace when you believed. And you can't take credit for this; it is a gift from God. Salvation is not a reward for the good things we have done, so none of us can boast about it. For we are God's masterpiece. He has created us anew in Christ Jesus, so we can do the good things he planned for us long ago.
> —EPHESIANS 2:4–10, NLT

3. And in Peter's first letter he tells us who we are:

> You are a chosen people. You are royal priests, a holy nation, God's very own possession. As a result, you can show others the goodness of God, for he called you out of the darkness into his wonderful light.
> —1 Peter 2:9–10, NLT

These passages from the Bible may be new to you, or you may have heard these truths and verses before. You even may have memorized them, but do you believe them, really believe them? Many of us struggle to believe the magnificent things God says about those He loves, but don't give up the fight. Ask God to make them real to you, undeniably, wonderfully real.

Who we declare ourselves to be matters. It determines why we do what we do; it provides a solid foundation when we take risks or hit turbulence in our health, families, or careers; and it has a profound impact on those around us. They're watching, and they can tell if we're selfish or generous, worried or at peace. We're leaving them a legacy, hopefully of grace and strength. This may be the biggest tombstone test of all.

I've truly come to believe, it's better to give than to receive. When that value takes root in our lives, we gladly and generously give our time, hearts, knowledge, skills, and wisdom. We have the unmitigated joy of seeing our input have terrific results in the lives of others, which gives us genuine delight.

A Surprising Declaration

Declarations are statements of who we are, what we want, and what we're committed to doing to achieve those results. We can declare our intentions in all the domains (though trying to tackle them all at once can be overwhelming). I've made countless declarations since I began implementing the principles of The Results Tree, but the most dramatic one came before I learned these concepts. In March of 2008 I was studying foreign policy at the Naval Postgraduate School in Monterey, California. One day, as I mentioned, my buddy Jack came to me out of the blue and asked if I wanted to attend a leadership training course with him over several weekends in Las Vegas. In spite of how busy I was, I jumped at the chance. So I arranged to miss class on Friday and flew to Vegas after class on Thursday.

The first weekend was about self-awareness. The exercises we participated in helped us peel back the layers of self-deception, uncover who we really are, and get in touch with our desires and motivations on a deep level. It was during this first weekend that I realized I didn't love myself, as I described in chapter 1. It was a decision I made about myself at a very early age, which had remained deeply buried and had shadowed nearly every choice in my life until that day. This realization was a watershed, a turning point in my life, that opened the door to new possibilities and a chance to make new empowering and positive declarations.

The second session, about ten days later, went much deeper and gave me the opportunity to break through my self-limiting beliefs, the excuses I used to avoid risks, such as "I'm not smart enough," "I'm not skilled enough," "I'm not important," and "I don't deserve to be loved." The longer and deeper I looked, the more I saw these cancerous beliefs were everywhere, and it was then that I committed to changing.

We then launched into the third level of the program, where we put all we had learned to work in the real world. For the next ninety days we had a professional coach who helped each of us compose a strategic plan with weekly SMART goals. Our coach and others on the team held us accountable and encouraged us to reach our goals. When we were off track, we examined what was out of alignment, redeclared our goals, and began again. One of my goals was to lose weight. I began at 210 and got down to 183. It wasn't enough to wish the weight would fall off. I had to take committed action every day and hold myself accountable. I knew whether I was moving toward my goal, and everybody else knew it too. During those three months I retired $20,000 in debt and took steps to repair my relationship with my dad. It was a monumental ninety days!

I found this third-level process so valuable that I volunteered to be one of the coaches for the next class. This allowed me to pay it forward to others who were just beginning their journey of discovery and personal growth. During the second weekend of the program Stacy, my coach (who was still coaching me and continues to coach me to this day), gave me an assignment: "By noon tomorrow, send me a description of your perfect woman."

Even though I didn't understand how the assignment fit into a leadership program, I immediately said, "Yes ma'am," because I had, and have, the greatest admiration for Stacy. She is one of the wisest, strongest people I've ever met. If she thought describing the woman of my dreams would be a good exercise for me, I'd do it. Once I gave my word, I was 100 percent committed to following through, because keeping promises to myself and others had by that point become one of the pillars of my own journey of personal transformation.

Months earlier, when I showed up for the first weekend of my own journey, I had made a series of commitments to be impeccable with my word: to be faithful to my girlfriend, cut back on my drinking and gambling, and be a more responsible person in all areas of my life. This process was a rocky one, with many starts, stops, and do-overs. With practice, reflection on the results, and redeclaration, I made measured improvement.

Now I had committed myself to an assignment that had to be completed by noon the next day, along with checking out of my hotel, getting to the airport, and catching my morning flight back to San Jose, and as usual I procrastinated, thinking it over, wanting what I wrote to be perfect. So I still hadn't written the description of my ideal woman when I landed in San Jose.

When I got off the plane, my friend Lisa was there to take me to my car. Neither of us needed to be anywhere soon, so we grabbed some coffee and chatted for a while. As we talked, I realized time was ticking on Stacy's assignment. I said, "Excuse me for a minute. I need to send a quick note to my coach." I grabbed my BlackBerry and hurriedly listed a bunch of characteristics for my perfect woman. When I finished, I hit "send." I turned to Lisa and asked, "Do you want to hear a description of my perfect woman?" Is there a woman on earth who would say no? Her eyes lit up, and she said, "Yes, of course!" I read the text:

> 5 feet, 10 inches, blonde, great figure, smart, happy, strong, loving, BALANCED, fun, classy, witty, educated, worldly, independent, gets me and loves me, good communicator, adventurous, nurturing, sexy, politically active, and transformational. How's that for a start?

Without missing a beat, Lisa almost shouted, "That's my best friend, Kristie!"

That night, October 20, 2008, Kristie and I talked on the phone for the first time. As we got to know each other, both of us wanted to pursue a relationship, but I quickly realized all my commitments from the leadership training class would be severely tested. What would it mean for me to be me, without carefully managing my image? I declared to Kristie that I'd be honest with her, but would I be willing to tell her I was deeply in debt and had herpes? Kristie lived in Hollywood and worked in the entertainment industry. What would she think of a guy on a fixed military salary? She attended A-list parties and movie premieres; my parties were beer and a cheese tray from Costco.

I knew I had to tell her. I'd come too far in my personal commitment to integrity to conveniently forget any hard truths that could derail our relationship. If we were to be together, Kristie needed to know everything. I told her, and she didn't run for the door. I'll be forever grateful for her kindness in those moments when I risked everything to tell her the truth.

Newton's first law of motion tells us that a body at rest stays at rest and a body in motion stays in motion unless acted upon by an outside force. The same principle applies in our lives: Transformation doesn't happen until we move, especially toward what we perceive as hard.

Growth begins when we summon the courage to face what we'd rather avoid. I've found, time and again, that when I've taken brave steps toward the hard thing, a divine force often redirects me toward what God truly intended for me to address. That redirection never comes until I'm willing to act with courage.

Hiding from the truth keeps us stuck. As long as we play the victim, deny our pain, make excuses, or blame others, we remain motionless. The moment we speak the truth, boldly and honestly, we begin moving forward. The law of motion is spiritual too: Integrity creates momentum.

Stepping into the unknown is risky. We can't control how others will respond or what consequences may follow. We gain something greater:

authenticity, growth, and the chance to live in alignment with who we are meant to be.

I can list many types of declarations, but living in honesty and integrity, with myself and others, may be the most important to me. No more games, no more masks, no more being a chameleon, changing colors depending on who's in front of me. Harbored secrets and private fears no longer dominate my thoughts and limit my actions.

Declarations aren't just words on a page we can quickly forget. They represent commitments to a better trajectory, richer relationships, and bold steps toward a vision of an incredible future.

Check out the Vision Engine (VSN NGN), an AI-powered interactive tool designed to help you clarify your vision, align your goals, and chart your next steps.

EXERCISES
Clarifying Intentions

Look at the list of the narrative of the inner critic on page 110. Do any of these sound familiar? Are there others that you've heard?

_____
_____
_____

How do you think these caustic voices have affected your self-image, your willingness to take risks, and your relationships?

_____
_____
_____

Now look at the list of affirmations starting on page 111. Which ones touch your heart?

_____
_____
_____

It's time to distill your vision into a single statement for portability. As you work on this, use your beginner's mind to answer the following questions again as if for the first time.

Reflect on Your Core Values

List adjectives that answer the question "What matters most to me in life?" Examples: Integrity, faith, growth, freedom, love, courage, service, etc.

_____

_____

_____

Identify Your Life's Purpose

Answer, "What impact do I want to make?" Think about the people you want to serve or the legacy you want to leave.

_____

_____

_____

Visualize Your Future Self

Ask, "Who am I becoming? What does my best, most authentic life look like?" Picture your ideal day, your character, your influence, and your joy. What are you committed to bringing forth from within so that you live a life you're proud of?

_____

_____

_____

Start with a Strong Verb

Use language that inspires action and ownership. Examples: Create, lead, build, live, love, serve, restore, empower, inspire, heal, guide, etc.

_____

_____

_____

Keep It Clear, Bold, and Personal

Avoid vague or passive phrases. Speak from your heart, to your future.

Sample Vision Statements

- Create beauty, give generously, and steward influence for lasting impact.
- Live fully, love deeply, lead boldly, and empower others to do the same.
- Inspire healing, growth, and purpose through faith, compassion, and courageous action.
- Live creatively, give boldly, and build a legacy of meaningful change.
- Build a life rooted in truth, driven by purpose, and overflowing with grace.
- Inspire through art, lead with generosity, and multiply good in the world.
- Create freedom and impact by living with clarity, integrity, and unshakable faith.
- Live with bold faith, lead with integrity, and empower others to rise into purpose.

Now boldly, freely bring all you have written into your own vision statement (in fifteen words or fewer). When you are done, pause and reflect, and imagine what your life may look like in ten, twenty, or fifty years with this as the soil in which your Results Tree takes root. Be gentle and kind with yourself. This is a win.

_____

_____

_____

Chapter 5

COMMITTED ACTION
Choose—Now!

You don't have to believe in your entire journey. Just believe in the next step.

ED MYLETT

A tree is consistent. It grows in a slow, steady process through the seasons. The rings show how long it has been alive and are a record of good years and lean years. In the winter cold it can look absolutely dead, but it's waiting with stored energy for a new season of growth. Every tree in the forest has endured cold and heat, drought and rain, and is dependent on its roots and the soil.

In September 2019 I was with my good friend Michael on a mountain near Las Vegas, getting ready to lead an exercise in risking and trust that was part of our leadership training. To test our equipment, I put on a climbing harness and climbing shoes and got ready to lean out over a cliff with a one-hundred-foot drop directly below me. The only things

COMMITTED ACTION

that would keep me from falling to my death on the rocks below were the two ropes attached to my climbing harness and securely tied to two trees to my right and my left, and a third rope clipped into the harness that Michael held in his hands behind me. I stepped up to the edge, planted my feet, and looked down at the rocks below. Even though I knew intellectually that I was safe, my heart was pounding in my chest, and I was breathing hard.

When my toes touched the edge, I made a declaration: "My name is Gabriel Griess. I freely choose this event. To me it represents letting go of my childish ways and stepping into my manhood." Then I planted my feet and began to lean out over nothing, empty space, with only the rocks below. Michael slowly payed out the rope. I leaned out farther and farther until I was almost horizontal, supported by my climbing harness and the rope and my feet pushing down on the edge of the cliff. I arched my back and looked out at the mountains in the distance and up at the sky, and shouted out a cry of gratitude to God. It was a life-changing moment in which all my fear of trusting myself and trusting other men vanished.

Then I called to Michael: "Pull me back."

Michael had been holding the rope tight, and now he started pulling me back up. From the top of the cliff I heard grunting and hard breathing. Michael was in the best shape of anyone I'd ever known, but since we were friends, I took this opportunity to razz him a little. "Hey, Michael, what's the problem? Not strong enough today?" If our roles had been reversed, it would have been more reasonable: I weighed about 235; Michael topped out at 160 after a big steak dinner with a couple of rocks in his pockets.

I couldn't see him, but I heard him reply, "How much do you weigh?"

"Oh, so it's on me, huh?"

He was making a little progress pulling me back in, and a few seconds later I could hear him straining on the rope. He gasped, "In case you didn't hear me, I asked, 'How much do you weigh?'"

"Yeah, I'm a little overweight."

"And the number is?"

"Oh, about 235."

Finally, he got me back on my feet. We stood and looked out at the mountains.

Now that he wasn't straining to pull and talk at the same time, Michael asked, "How much do you *want* to weigh?"

"I'd like to live under 200."

Without missing a beat, he asked, "By when?"

To Michael this was the concrete application of my declaration to give up childish ways and live a responsible life. I had told him my goal; now he asked for a deadline.

"By March."

Michael smiled, "OK, send me a picture of a scale with you standing on it every Monday until then." Accountability—you gotta have it.

Of course, losing weight, like most goals, isn't accomplished in a perfectly straight line. There are ups and downs, like Saturday afternoon football games, Thanksgiving, Christmas, office parties, and every other kind of holiday festivity when there's plenty of food and adult beverages. Every week, I talked to Michael to share when I had been disciplined and when I wasn't as rigorous as I should have (and could have) been. I soon discovered that if I'm serious about a goal, a lot of things that seemed vital before become extraneous, or maybe hindrances, such as grabbing something at a drive-through, munching on snacks, eating too much ice cream, getting second (and third) helpings, skipping a meal and "making up for it" with a king's feast, and plenty more.

On January 1, 2024, I sent Michael a picture of my bare feet on a scale that read 197. You might remark, "Gabriel, do you mean it took you more than four years?"

Yes, it did, but I made progress all along the way. Actually, it's a bit more complicated. By January 2020 I weighed 210, and in March, my target date, I was at 204. Pretty darn close! You might remember a little blip that changed the lifestyles of a lot of people in 2020: COVID-19. It was less convenient to exercise because gyms were closed, I worked from home a lot, and (surprise!) our home has a refrigerator. And the store has

Milk Duds, a wide assortment of candy bars, plenty of desserts, and . . . You get the idea. I wasn't one of those people who came out of COVID as a sinewy, wiry warrior. I was on the other side of the curve. Let's also be honest, in the world of accountability all these are excuses and none of them excuse my behavior. I made choices that didn't align with my vision for my life. I made something else more important than my health and my commitment to myself and my friend.

My point is that declarations set our goals, but clear intention and committed action are required to reach them. Our most important goals seldom happen quickly. We need tenacity over time to see the results. Did I hit the goal I set with Michael? No. Was I close? Yes. Did I give up? Hmm, yes and no. I made some bad choices along the way, but generally, I kept the goal in front of me. The human animal is incredibly creative and dedicated to finding ways to bail on commitments, and we'll rationalize it in a way that makes sure others say something like, "Oh, that makes total sense," or, "I understand why that goal became impossible to reach." Be careful of these people. They want to be able to tell you about things that are important to them, and then when it gets tough, they want you to support them in quitting and not feeling bad about it

Update: At the time I was writing this chapter, I was back in the groove, moving from 205 to sub-200. Controlling my weight and having good health is an important goal that requires a lifestyle change, but it's worth it because Kristie and I are committed to holding our great-grandbabies. Can we make it? I'll be about one hundred when they are born, and I'm so excited to look into their eyes and hold their little hands. That's my goal; that's my commitment; that's my passion.

Eight Reasons We Bail

We can put the reasons we quit our goals into a few broad categories:

1. Our vision is fuzzy.

When our goals aren't specific and measurable, it's easy to give up. They may not be rooted in a compelling vision, and they may not be connected to an important why. Amorphous goals are pretty worthless. Fuzzy visions are half-baked. I could have told Michael, "Yeah, it would be nice to be under 200 pounds someday," but that statement would have revealed that I had very little passion or drive to get there.

When I told Michael my goal, I soon surrounded it with plenty of whys: I can get off my meds for blood pressure, I'll have more energy to play with my kids, my joints won't hurt, I'll have better sex, and it's more likely that I'll be around to hang out with my grandchildren. All those are important to me, more important than a few moments of pleasure eating candy bars and ice cream.

One of Stephen Covey's seven habits of highly effective people is this succinct but crucial concept: "Start with the end in mind." He uses a scene from Alice in Wonderland to illustrate the point:

One day Alice came to a fork in the road and saw a Cheshire cat in a tree. "Which road do I take?" she asked.

"Where do you want to go?" was his response.

"I don't know," Alice answered.

"Then," said the cat, "it doesn't matter."[37]

The problem isn't that we're weak. The problem is we're unclear. And when we're unclear, we chase comfort instead of commitment.

2. **We deceive ourselves.**

We boldly declare our goals, sometimes even with ceremony and conviction, but often we don't truly own them. Why? Because our intentions aren't clear and our desire isn't burning. Deep down we haven't decided that the goal is worth the discomfort, sacrifice, or change it demands. We might not say it out loud, but our actions reveal the truth: "That would be nice, but other things matter more right now."

"All change is not growth, as all movement is not forward."
ELLEN GLASGOW

I've been there. For me, it was a bowl of ice cream that won out over discipline, an excuse that felt better than a workout, a hundred little moments where comfort beat commitment. But the goal still meant something, so I kept coming back. That's what made the difference.

The truth is, people who abandon their goals often haven't fully counted the cost, not just the cost of pursuing the goal but the cost of *not* pursuing it. The personal cost. The relational cost. The emotional and even spiritual cost. Without that clarity, we're just making wishes, not setting goals.

We say we want to lose weight, but we want the snack more. We say we want to be debt-free, but we keep clicking "add to cart." We say our family matters most, but it's easier to scroll, stream, or talk to someone who doesn't challenge us to grow than it is to spend quality time with our partner or our kids.

3. **It takes too long.**

We live in a culture of instant results, in practically every area of our lives. With a few clicks we can order almost anything and have it delivered tomorrow (if not today). We have drive-through restaurants, and we used to use drive-through banking before we could make transactions in the palms of our hands from our smartphones. We've learned that we don't have to wait, and we think that delayed gratification is for suckers. When we set an important goal, it's countercultural to remain tenacious over time. It's easier to give up and focus our attention on something that gives us an immediate thrill or relief.

Pursuing meaningful results is hard work. We might hear stories of someone who achieved great success very quickly, but I'm always suspicious about these accounts. Usually, the person had spent years studying, working, and testing, and when "it worked," the incredible results seemed like an overnight success, but they weren't. True progress takes practice, consistent, intentional, often unglamorous effort. As Malcolm Gladwell famously wrote, "It takes 10,000 hours of intensive practice to achieve mastery of complex skills."[38] That kind of commitment isn't about hype; it's about daily decisions that align with a bigger vision.

4. We allow our vision to be squashed.

There's a wise observation that says our lives are shaped by the five people we spend the most time with. If my vision is to become a better husband and father and one of my goals is to stop drinking, I am going to struggle if my five closest friends head to the bar every afternoon after work. If I've committed to being more responsible with money and I've created a clear plan to spend less and save more, I will feel constant pressure if those around me are always chasing the newest gadgets, cars, or luxury vacations, and talking about it nonstop.

This is a tough one. It often requires us to take an honest look at the influence others are having on us and consider making some necessary adjustments. I am not saying we need to cut people out of our lives just because they don't support our goals. If someone consistently models self-indulgence or a lack of discipline, we may need to see them less often, meet in different settings, or establish boundaries that protect our vision.

Instead of hanging out in places that feed old habits, we can choose different environments. For example, we can play pickleball or golf, volunteer at a nonprofit, meet for coffee, or explore any of the thousand other ways to connect that don't compromise who we are becoming.

5. We have too many goals.

Many of us are into multitasking, and we're proud of ourselves for keeping so many balls in the air. Experts are starting to realize this is a recipe for mediocrity. To achieve excellence in any domain, it's more effective to focus on a few truly important goals and leave others until later. Momentum Partners explains the problem: "Everything feels urgent. Your day-to-day obligations compete with your goals, your goals compete with each other, and you're left juggling it all (while feeling defeated and overwhelmed)." And a recommended solution: "Have fewer goals. Seriously. One of the things preventing you from reaching any one goal is all your other goals. Focus on a few at a time. Select three, at most five, and ignore the ten other things you think you need to achieve. You'll get to them soon enough."[39]

6. The goal is unrealistic.

Some people get fired up and set goals that are unrealistic. They're passionate and excited, and they tell everyone who will listen how they'll get there, but sooner or later (often sooner), they hit a wall. If I'd set my weight goal at 165, I would have given up at some point because that number isn't realistic for my height and shape. I'm not an Olympic distance runner. I was at 165 in my twenties, and I was all spring steel and rawhide, very little fat at all. My commitment and vision is to live at a weight that supports my long-term health.

7. We aren't flexible and adaptable.

I'm not an artist, but I'd bet that every painter, sculptor, dancer, architect, photographer, and artist of every other stripe has an evolving dream for their art and themselves. It's not a flaw that your dream evolves and changes over time. That's a sign that you're alive and working hard to pursue the results! In the crucible of stating clear intentions and taking committed action, we gain new insights and acquire new skills. We can change without growing, but growth always involves change. Don't be surprised if your vision evolves, your goals change from one season of life to the next, and your committed action leads to results you hadn't imagined in the past.

8. Failure becomes a brick wall across our paths.

Wise people realize that they win some and lose some. The important thing is to stay in the game. Failure may be discouraging, but a hopeful perspective takes the sting out of it. In an article in *Inc.*, Nicolas Cole explains:

> The best goal-setters know that failure is nothing more than a lesson in disguise. . . . Those that give up on their goals, however, treat failure as a label. "I've failed," they repeat to themselves over and over, entirely missing the opportunity right in front of their eyes. It's only a failure if you see it that way. To everyone else succeeding, it's nothing more than a hard-earned lesson.[40]

When you experience what looks like major setbacks, remember the story of the Chinese farmer and say, "We'll see."

Passion Is Vital

Failure can be a terrific opportunity to evaluate, well, everything. It's wise to take a long, hard look at your vision. Is it something you're really passionate about? Are your goals rooted in your vision? And then look at your resources of time, skills, and supporters. Did you have enough to do the job right? My friend Guy Wells gave this clear advice: "If I find myself rowing upstream, I just turn around and paddle downriver." Great leadership—at home, at work, and in every kind of organization—is driven by passion. If we want our people to be passionate and committed, we need to first look in the mirror to see if we live each day with passion and are enjoying this journey called life. Leaders and parents who lack passion will have followers and children who lack commitment to a cause bigger than themselves. The old saying about wolves is true: "The speed of the leader is the speed of the pack." If you're frustrated by the poor attitude, inferior work ethic, energy, and commitment of the people around you, wake up. They may be following your example!

The word *passion* originated in the first century, during the time of Christ. It was used to describe His suffering on the cross. It means being willing to suffer for something or someone you love. This kind of commitment causes us to show up early, stay late, find solutions, bring out the best in everyone, and get the job done.[41] One of my heroes is Gen. Douglas MacArthur, who understood the nature of suffering for a cause. He said, "On the fields of friendly strife are sown the seeds that on other days, on other fields will bear the fruits of victory."[42] You've probably heard or read Theodore Roosevelt's quote about tenacity many times, but perhaps you haven't seen the most famous part in context. When he was in Paris on April 23, 1910, at the Sorbonne, Roosevelt delivered a speech in his soaring oratorical style to "ministers in court dress, army and navy officers in full uniform, nine hundred students, and an audience of two thousand ticketholders."[43] The speech was titled "Citizenship in a Republic" but is informally and popularly known as "The Man in the Arena." Roosevelt's challenge to his audience (and to us) sounded like this:

> It is not the critic who counts; not the man who points out how the strong man stumbles, or where the doer of deeds could have done them better. The credit belongs to the man who is actually in the arena, whose face is marred by dust and sweat and blood; who strives valiantly; who errs, who comes short again and again, because there is no effort without error and shortcoming; but who does actually strive to do the deeds; who knows great enthusiasms, the great devotions; who spends himself in a worthy cause; who at the best knows in the end the triumph of high achievement, and who at the worst, if he fails, at least fails while daring greatly, so that his place shall never be with those cold and timid souls who neither know victory nor defeat.[44]

This is as powerful and clear a description of the impact of passion as I've ever read. Yes, familiarity can blunt any idea, but Roosevelt reminds us that drive is essential to carry us through to reach our goals.

This Moment

Successful people know they have amazing opportunities and significant risks in every choice. The past gives them knowledge and experience, and their dreams paint a picture of the future, but they live in the present, this time, this moment, this decision to move forward or back away. Let me put it another way: Our past is the preface to the present, and the present is the preface to the future, but this is the only moment when we can make decisions and take committed action.

"You will either step forward into growth or you will step back into safety."
ABRAHAM MASLOW

As we've seen, we can come up with a lot of reasons to avoid risk, but in playing it safe, we'll miss the opportunity. If we wait for everything to be perfect, we'll stay stuck in the fear of making a mistake. It recently happened to me.

My friend Smokey called and left a message with wonderful news: He had a girlfriend, and he was really excited about the relationship. I could have called him back right away, but I wanted to find a time when Kristie and I could both be on the call. Four weeks later I still hadn't called to celebrate with my friend. When I realized how long it had been, I called and left a message: "Hey, man, I'm so sorry it has taken so long to get back to you. Kristie and I wanted to be on the phone to congratulate you together, but it just hasn't worked out. I didn't want another day to pass before I let you know how happy we are for you." I could have said the same thing (except for the part about being sorry) minutes after I heard his message, but I kept waiting for the perfect scenario I had in mind, one that never happened. He called me back a few minutes after I left the message, and we had a terrific conversation.

Life is a chain of ordinary moments, each one a fork in the road. Most of the time, the choice feels small, harmless, easy to shrug off. When added up, those choices carve a path that either draws us closer to our vision or quietly drags us away from it.

Here are a few moments that don't look dangerous but carry more power than we admit:

1. "The $300 fishing rod is calling my name . . . even though $20,000 of debt already sits on my shoulders."
2. "It's late, and I'm alone. No one will know what I click on tonight . . . but I will."
3. "My devotional always steadies me, but right now the snooze button whispers louder."
4. "I'm exhausted. Home should be refuge, but instead of connection I want silence. It feels easier to withdraw."
5. "This pie is perfect. One more slice won't matter, except I know it does."
6. "I didn't tell a lie . . . just left out the details that would make me look weak. But now I'm hiding behind half-truths."
7. "You want closeness, but I don't. The distance between us grows in the quiet."
8. "The gym is crowded, the air stale, and every excuse feels stronger than my will."

These are the invisible battlefields of the everyday. Not dramatic, not catastrophic, but quietly decisive. Every choice either strengthens discipline or weakens it. Every small yes to comfort over commitment puts space between us and the vision we said we were committed to.

You get the idea. One of our problems is that we have difficulty being present in the moment and focusing on the decision that needs to be made here and now. We act without being fully aware of the consequences of our actions. Why? Probably for many reasons, but surely one is that we live with constant intentional distractions. Linda Stone, formerly of Apple and Microsoft, coined the term *continuous partial attention* to describe the constant distractions of our communication devices. She writes:

> To pay continuous partial attention is to pay partial attention—CONTINUOUSLY. It is motivated by a desire to be a LIVE node on the network. Another way of saying this is that we want to connect and be connected. We want to effectively scan for opportunity and optimize for the best opportunities, activities, and contacts, in any given moment. To be busy, to be connected, is to be alive, to be recognized, and to matter. We pay continuous partial attention in an effort NOT TO MISS ANYTHING. It is an always-on, anywhere, anytime, anyplace behavior that involves an artificial sense of constant crisis. We are always in high alert when we pay continuous partial attention. This artificial sense of constant crisis is more typical of continuous partial attention than it is of multi-tasking.[45]

Sound familiar? Of course it does. It's the way many of us live all day, every day, unless we take steps to eliminate the distractions or at least minimize them. Focused effort is required to live in the present and avoid distractions, but it always seems something or someone is more important than being fully present in the moment. Many of us live with pervasive FOMO, fear of missing out. We don't want to miss anything, but the result is that we miss the joy and meaning that's only available in the present moment. We find all kinds of excuses to multitask, including, "I have too much to do," "It won't get done if I don't do it," and, "I'm committed to excellence." When things inevitably fall through the cracks, we're defensive, we blame anyone and everyone else, and we complain that no one understands how hard we're trying. It's possible to be completely focused on the present. For instance, as I'm writing this chapter, my day job hasn't taken a break. There are deadlines, deals, and decisions crying for my attention. I turned off my phone, took off my Apple watch, and carved out time to fully concentrate on writing.

Tenacity Over Time

When I showed up at the Air Force Academy as a new cadet, I was ushered into Arnold Hall with the other 1,499 men and women entering the class of '95. I don't remember a lot of what was said in that orientation, but one statement hit me like a sledgehammer: "Look to your left. Look to your right. In four years one of you won't be here." Our graduating class was 970 people, so a little more than one-third of the highly qualified cadets didn't make it.

The reasons for not completing the academy were as individual as the people who left. My dear friend Troy stepped away before our junior year because his dream was to become a doctor. The Air Force couldn't guarantee him a medical school slot, and he knew his vision for his life was sharper, more focused, and more compelling than staying. His decision was anything but easy—he gave up security and financial stability, and faced criticism—but today he's a physician in Chicago with a beautiful family.

Others left because they realized the dream they were pursuing wasn't really their own. Some felt the pressure of carrying a family legacy of service, but legacy alone can't carry the weight of purpose. Others discovered that academy life didn't match the lifestyle they imagined for themselves, or that their high school habits hadn't prepared them for the academy's academic rigor.

These stories don't contradict the call to perseverance; they highlight something important: Grit must be anchored in the right vision. Perseverance without purpose can lead to burnout or regret, but perseverance with clarity of calling leads to impact and fulfillment. The cadets who stayed and thrived knew deep down that being an officer was their purpose. The ones who left did so not because they were weak but because they had the courage to admit their vision lay elsewhere. Both paths required bravery.

When we're pursuing a goal rooted in our vision, sometimes the road gets hard, motivation starts to fade, and quitting starts to sound reasonable. When that happens, and it can happen to the best of us, the key is to simply make the right decision in this moment, then the next, and the next. Progress isn't about constant inspiration; it's about consistent choice. As Angela Duckworth writes in *Grit: The Power of Passion and Perseverance*:

> Why were the highly accomplished so dogged in their pursuits? For most, there was no realistic expectation of ever catching up to their ambitions.... They wouldn't dream of giving up....
> No matter the domain, the highly successful had a kind of ferocious determination that played out in two ways. First, these exemplars were usually resilient and hardworking. Second, they knew in a very, very deep way what it was they wanted. The not only had determination, they had direction.
> It was this combination of passion and perseverance that made high achievers special. In a word, they had grit.[46]

When You Fail

It's not about if you fail, but when. People who are attempting great things invariably experience big setbacks. It's part of the territory. It may be a bit trite, but it's true: *The road to success is paved with lessons learned through failure,* and the smartest among us learn from other people's failures. Many people are so afraid to fail that they construct lives specifically designed to avoid any mess-ups. They live in a twilight zone of trying to find meaning from the mundane. Other people live for the adrenaline rush of always being on the edge of catastrophe. High risks make them feel alive, but the people around them either hang on tight, drop off because they can't take the constant risks, or get crushed under high expectations. Successful people learn to take the perspective "Do your best, expect mixed results, and celebrate the opportunity to learn life's most valuable lessons when you fail."

The brilliant inventor and artist Leonardo da Vinci observed, "It had long since come to my attention that people of accomplishment rarely sat back and let things happen to them. They went out and happened to things."[47]

Chris Hemsworth, in a refreshingly honest reflection on his role in *Thor: Love and Thunder*, admitted: "I got caught up in the improv and the wackiness, and I became a parody of myself."[48] Despite years of blockbuster hits and critical acclaim, he wasn't immune to the pressures of performance and the sting of critique.

Similarly, actor, comedian, and producer Chris Hardwick wrote that recovering from failure makes people memorable: "No human ever became interesting by not failing. The more you fail and recover and improve, the better you are as a person. Ever meet someone who's always had everything work out for them with zero struggle? They usually have the depth of a puddle. Or they don't exist."[49]

Leadership expert Napoleon Hill observes, "Most great people have attained their greatest success just one step beyond their greatest failure."[50]

When we fail, we gain experience and insights we didn't have the day before. Don't beat yourself up. Be kind to yourself, full of grace and patience. How would you treat someone you love who failed? Treat yourself the same way. Some of us have internalized voices from the past that told us we were stupid and would never make it in life. Those voices scream at us at the slightest mistake, even when we didn't make a mistake. When this happens, past wounds have been weaponized to shoot us down today. We need a far better internal narrative to empower us instead of torturing ourselves. See the list of positive affirmations in chapter 4.

What do we learn from our failures? Perhaps many different things. Sometimes we realize our vision wasn't rooted in our purpose, so we didn't have the clarity and commitment required to follow through. Or maybe a goal was unrealistic, we didn't have adequate resources, we didn't have connections with people who could help us, or something unforeseen got in the way.

Failure shows us places where we need to think more deeply, plan more effectively, grow in areas we've neglected, mend strained relationships, and take 100 percent responsibility for our part in any endeavor. For me the nonrelational goals are pretty easy to set and move toward: my weight, finances, time management, and so on. Relationships require more than good planning and determination. They call out my heart and force me to be vulnerable, to engage when I want to run away, and to be kind when it would be easy to be unkind. I have the opportunity to take responsibility for who I've been to the people around me, own my broken agreements, and face up to my lapses in compassion.

For years my relationship with my dad as an adult was distant. We weren't estranged—I was in the Air Force, and he was a busy professional—but we weren't close either. I didn't make the effort to know him better. We never carved out time for just the two of us to be together as men. No fishing trips. No shared vacations. And rarely did we talk about what truly mattered to either of us.

"Success is walking from failure to failure with no loss of enthusiasm."
WINSTON CHURCHILL

On a scale of one to ten, our connection hovered around a five or six, not hostile, just quiet, unengaged, and emotionally shallow. I'm not sure when the drift began, but over time the gap between us started to feel like too much to bridge.

If I'm being honest, I carried shame. Deep down I knew parts of how I was living weren't aligned with the grounded faith he had modeled for me as a child. That disconnect made it even harder to engage. I tried reaching out a few times over the years, but the conversations didn't land, and nothing really changed.

Then, a few years ago, a sobering thought came over me: One day I would be standing beside his grave. Would I have done enough? Would I live with the regret of not trying harder? That moment broke through my hesitation. I stopped focusing on what wasn't working and started asking what *I* could do differently. I admitted my part in the distance between my dad and me. I chose to show up; to invest my time, my heart, and my presence; and to start rebuilding a bridge that had been left untended for far too long.

I've heard stories of remarkable reconciliation. My friend James had been estranged from his brother for his whole life. Even when they were boys, his brother was cruel to him, stole from him, and did his best to make his life miserable. As an adult, James made several attempts to move toward his brother, but he was rejected each time. Finally, when both of them were old men, his brother called to say, "I'm dying, and I want to make things right." He apologized to James and asked for forgiveness.

As James had surrendered and done the hard work of forgiving for many years, it was a prayer come true to share his forgiveness with his brother.

Things don't always work out that way. I know many people who would love to mend a broken relationship, but the other person won't have it. The longing doesn't go away, even as we grieve the loss of a closeness we crave. We live with a hole in our hearts, but we don't need to feel guilty. In Paul's letter to the Christians in Rome he gave them clear instructions: "Bless those who persecute you; bless and do not curse. . . . Do not repay anyone evil for evil. Be careful to do what is right in the eyes of everyone. If it is possible, as far as it depends on you, live at peace with everyone" (Rom. 12:14, 17–18). Paul doesn't stop there. He recognizes that our normal human response when someone hurts us is to get even, to pay them back at least as much as they've hurt us. Forgiveness isn't a commodity; it's a frame of mind. It absorbs the pain instead of inflicting pain, and it hurts because it runs contrary to our God-given sense of justice. We want people to pay for what they've done! Paul addresses our passion for justice:

> Do not take revenge, my dear friends, but leave room for God's wrath, for it is written: "It is mine to avenge; I will repay," says the Lord. On the contrary: "If your enemy is hungry, feed him; if he is thirsty, give him something to drink. In doing this, you will heap burning coals on his head." Do not be overcome by evil but overcome evil with good.
> —ROMANS 12:19–21

When we're tempted to take revenge, either overtly by harming them or covertly by talking about someone behind their back, we need to remember that God is the righteous judge, not us. Can we trust Him to be just and fair to the person who hurt us? If not, we'll take justice into our hands and make that person suffer. If we can trust someone who treated us unfairly, we can put that person in the hands of God and choose to forgive, even if the person isn't sorry and hasn't changed. We can bless them and refuse to harbor vengeance in our hearts. Author and pastor Lewis Smedes encourages us to be brutally honest about the hurt without excusing the person, without minimizing the offense, and not denying it even happened. He advises, "When we forgive evil we do not excuse it, we do not tolerate it, we do not smother it. We look the evil full in the face, call it what it is, let its horror shock and stun and enrage us, and only then do we forgive it."[51] When we refuse to forgive, our minds relive the scenes of the offense and imagine scenes of revenge. Smedes encourages us, "Vengeance is having a videotape planted in your soul that cannot be turned off. It plays the painful scene over and over again inside your mind.... And each time it plays you feel the clap of pain again.... Forgiving turns off the videotape of pained memory. Forgiving sets you free."[52]

100 Percent Responsible

Just as seeking revenge is a natural human impulse, so is blaming others when something goes wrong. How do people respond when we point the finger at them? The same way we do. They get defensive and start blaming us back.

We often think a fifty-fifty split of responsibility is fair, but in practice it doesn't lead to growth. Real transformation begins when we fully own our part in any situation. Not halfway. Not conditionally. Completely.

And when we do, something remarkable happens. Defensiveness fades. Conversations shift. Relationships open. Ownership creates space for healing, progress, and mutual respect. It's not about taking the blame for everything; it's about stepping fully into the only part we can control: our own choices, our own attitude, our own growth.

Not long ago we were late filing a paper required by a state where we do business. My business manager had sent me the DocuSign form by email, but I'd missed it. When she learned that I hadn't submitted it on time, she let me know. I searched my email files and found it. She had sent it in plenty of time. It was entirely my fault, and I told her, "This is on me. I blew it."

Her response was, "I could have reminded you. I could have sent another email, texted, or called you. I knew this was important. I'm sorry."

"No need to be sorry," I assured her. "This was entirely on me."

Could I have blamed her for not following up? Certainly. I might have felt powerful and dominant for a few minutes but at the expense of a valued relationship. I chose to absorb the responsibility, and it made our relationship even stronger.

This principle may be most powerful, and most needed, in marriage. Many couples function with something that resembles a business contract. Responsibilities—chores, finances, parenting, schedules—are divided. And for a while, it works, until one partner feels overwhelmed or falls short of an unspoken expectation.

That's when things begin to unravel.

The other person feels let down, overlooked, maybe even betrayed. Blame creeps in. "You're so selfish. You don't care. You never follow through." Harsh words or quiet resentment take the place of honest connection. The real problem often lies deeper. Much of the conflict stems from an implied and unspoken contract, expectations that were never clearly voiced.

Unexpressed expectations are premeditated resentments. When we expect something without ever communicating it, we are unknowingly planting seeds of frustration that will grow into bitterness.

When tension flares, most couples default to one of two destructive tracks: blowing up or shutting down. Blowing up looks like harsh tones, hurtful words, slammed doors, and wounded hearts. Shutting down is quieter but just as dangerous. Smiles might stay on the surface, but underneath, love is slowly replaced by distance, loneliness, and a quiet ache that goes unnamed.

Healing begins when even one person chooses a different response. When someone says, gently and sincerely, "That's my responsibility; I'll take care of it. No problem," something shifts. The temperature drops. Defenses lower. Grace and forgiveness start to move in. Kindness returns.

And in that space, humble, honest, and safe, something beautiful begins to grow again.

The principle of 100 percent responsibility applies to every relationship, in our families, at work, with our kids, our parents, our neighbors, and even strangers in line at the coffee shop. It's not limited to major life decisions. It shows up in ordinary, unexpected moments too. Let me take it to the limit. Say I park my car and go into a store, and while I'm inside, someone swerves and hits my car. What does it mean to be 100 percent responsible in that moment? It means I recognize I could have parked somewhere else, but I didn't. I could lash out at the driver, but I choose not to. I could tell everyone I know for the next three days how careless they were, but I let it go. No, I'm not responsible for their mistake. I *am* responsible for how I respond to the consequences. It's natural to get upset, but I still have a choice. My car is dented and scraped; that's a fact. In this moment, I choose to respond with respect and kindness. I choose to find the best path forward for both of us. That's what 100 percent responsibility looks like, not controlling the world around me but taking ownership of how I show up in it.

Taking a deeper look, 100 percent responsibility means recognizing that events are neutral and that I always have a choice in how I respond. If I choose to play the victim, get angry, blame others, or complain, I'm the one who suffers, not the person who hurt me, not the person who cut me off, not the one who failed me.

So the real question becomes, What do I want to experience?

If I want peace, if I want clarity, if I want to live aligned with my values, it means taking full responsibility, not because it's the morally superior thing to do or because it's what a "good" person would choose, but because it's how I shape the life I want to live. When I take responsibility for my reaction, I reclaim my power.

This is the shift from reacting to responding.

A reaction is automatic, emotional, and often rooted in fear. A response, on the other hand, creates a small but powerful space between the event and my choice. In that space, I can align with my vision, my purpose, and my values.

To respond is to be *responseable*, to own my ability to choose, even in the face of hard things.

Like all couples, Kristie and I don't always see eye to eye. We occasionally have different perspectives and desires around important issues. When calm conversations don't lead to agreement and the emotional temperature starts to rise, we lean on two simple mantras that bring us back to what matters most. One of us will say, "Remember, we're on the same team." Or sometimes we laugh and say, "We're in violent agreement," when we realize we're saying the same thing, just in different ways.

When tension enters any relationship, our natural response is often fight, flight, or freeze. If we train ourselves to pause and process the emotions and threatening thoughts that bubble up, we can move beyond reactivity. We can choose to respond with clarity and compassion, seeking to understand more than demanding to be understood.

That's when something powerful happens.

When one person takes 100 percent responsibility for their part and says, "That's on me. I'm sorry I reacted like that," the atmosphere shifts. The intensity softens. What felt like a battle becomes a conversation again. Two people find common ground and commit to treating each other with dignity and respect. (When all else fails, you can always have the conversation naked; that tends to lighten the mood.)

In a *Forbes* article titled "Why True Leaders Never Blame Others (or Circumstances)," ex-Microsoft executive John Rex explains, "The truth is, in *every* situation there are factors outside our control and factors *within* our control. I challenge you to find an exception.... Even the most dire circumstances offer elements that lie within your control. If someone locks you in a dungeon and throws away the key, many things will indeed be outside your control. Some will remain in your control. Most important among them is your ability to choose your response."[53]

Blaming other people does absolutely nothing constructive. Events are neutral. Accept reality, take responsibility, make a decision, and move on. Remember Viktor Frankl. If he could choose his reaction in a Nazi concentration camp, you and I are certainly able to choose our reaction to our day-to-day circumstances.

Accountability

Many of us like to think of ourselves as "rugged individualists," strong, self-reliant, able to make it on our own without help. In my experience that's an illusion. None of us get where we're going without support, encouragement, wise direction, and occasionally a well-timed motivational kick in the pants.

Not everyone has earned the right to be that kind of accountability partner. If you open the door to too many voices, you risk having your dreams crushed instead of refined. We do need one or two trusted people who are willing to set aside their fear of looking good and step up to speak the truth, gently, honestly, and with our best interest at heart.

Here's what I've learned: The right people tend to show up when we get clear about where we're going. When we define our vision, declare bold goals, and take those first real steps forward, something shifts. We begin to recognize the kind of mentor we need, and we become the kind of person a good mentor is drawn to.

As the old saying goes, "When the student is ready, the teacher appears."

So if you're waiting for the perfect guide before you begin, consider this: Clarity attracts help. Momentum draws support. Start moving toward what matters, and the right people will find you, or you'll be ready to find them.

When we seek a coach or mentor, we step into a double vetting process. We must discern whether the prospective mentor is someone we can trust, someone with the character, wisdom, and steadiness to hold space for our dreams, our fears, and our growth. And at the same time, they are evaluating us. Are we teachable? Do we have the humility and hunger to make the most of their time, insight, and investment?

Can a friend serve in this role? Possibly. Many friendships, while valuable, don't run deep enough. Some friends are content to keep things light—shared laughs, casual check-ins, surface-level support. There's nothing wrong with that. Mentoring requires more. It calls for honesty, accountability, and the willingness to wade into the deep water of what really matters.

For mentoring to be effective, two essential ingredients must be present: character and a framework.

By character I mean integrity, life experience, discernment, and a willingness to tell the truth in love. By framework I mean the coaching conversation is guided and intentional. It is an interaction centered around real growth, not just advice. Unsurprisingly, I believe that the person we choose as our mentor must be willing to bring us back over and over again to the essentials: vision, clear intentions, committed action, and results.

I'm blessed to have two people who play this part in my life's drama. One is my wife, Kristie, and the other is my best friend and business partner, Kevin, whom I met on June 27, 1991, when we had our heads shaved as we entered the Air Force Academy.

Frankly, we don't need a mentor or accountability partner for every goal. If a goal is small, bite-size, and easily doable, we can probably knock it out on our own. But goals like that rarely move the needle in our lives. They don't stir our hearts, stretch our limits, or call out our full potential.

And if we're honest, that's where mediocrity creeps in, not through failure but through aiming too low, through settling for goals that keep us busy but not bold, goals that keep us comfortable, not courageous.

But we weren't made for mediocrity. Deep down we want something more. We want excellence, not perfection but purpose-filled progress. We want to live in alignment with our vision, with clear intentions and meaningful results. That kind of life requires support. It requires someone wise and trustworthy to walk alongside us and challenge us to stay the course.

Depending on where you are in the journey, that person might be a peer, someone walking a similar path, starting from the same point. Together you can encourage each other, share truth, and hold each other accountable. That's the power of mutual partnership, and it's why support groups and recovery circles are so effective. Two people who are both in the fight can sharpen each other daily.

Or you may seek someone a few steps ahead, someone who's already navigated the path you're just stepping onto, someone who brings the insight and credibility of experience, someone who can help you avoid unnecessary setbacks and push you further than you thought you could go.

This is how excellence is built, step by step, together.

Don't settle. Choose excellence. Choose growth. And choose to walk with someone who will call you up, not just cheer you on.

Whatever structure you choose, never lose sight of your vision. You are writing your life's story right now with every decision, every word, every breath.

Key questions to consider are: What kind of impact are you making today? What will your legacy be? What will history say of your life? An exercise in appendix A will lead you through a deep examination of these questions.

Remember, eagles don't get their flight plans from chickens.

EXERCISES
Staying Committed

Looking back at your life, when have you felt most passionate about a goal? What did you do to pursue it?

_____
_____
_____

What usually helps you keep going when things get tough, and what has caused you to quit in the past?

_____
_____
_____

Think about your patterns: What excuses, distractions, or fears most often stop you from following through?

_____
_____
_____

What will keep you going this time? What matters more to you than short-term comfort or giving up?

_____
_____
_____

Who can you invite into your journey to encourage you, challenge you, and hold you accountable?

_____
_____
_____

Write down your top three goals. For each one, what possible roadblocks might you face, and how will you prepare to push through them?

1. _____
_____
_____
_____
_____
_____

2. _____
_____
_____
_____
_____
_____

3. _____
_____
_____
_____
_____

Chapter 6

RESULTS
The Life You Really Want

> *Make the Mental Image.... The Earnest Desire is the feeling, the Confident Expectation is the thought, and the Firm Demand is the will, and, as we have seen, feeling gives vitality to thought and the will holds it steadily until the law of Growth brings it into manifestation.*
> WHO NOT HOW BY DAN SULLIVAN WITH DR. BENJAMIN HARDY

You've planted the roots of your vision deep in solid ground. With clear intention, you've declared meaningful goals. With committed action, you've shown up again and again. Now it's time. You're living in your results.

Results aren't waiting somewhere far off in the future. They're already here, woven into your daily life. When you pursue your vision with clarity and integrity, results show up constantly. Sometimes they look like progress. Other times they arrive as feedback. Either way, they are always speaking, if you're paying attention.

156 THE RESULTS TREE

A clear vision gives you a clear lens. It allows you to see whether your life is aligned, and where growth is still needed. To sharpen that lens, ask yourself:

- » What's the condition of my closest relationships? Are they marked by encouragement and love, or by distance and tension?
- » Do I live with gratitude and hope, or do I dwell more on fear, worry, and what's missing?
- » Is my vision present in my daily thoughts and choices, or has it faded to the background?
- » Am I seeing real progress toward what matters most while avoiding the pitfalls of perfection?

» Is this vision truly mine? Do I own it, or does it just sound good on paper?
» Am I showing up consistently and courageously, even when it's uncomfortable?

Your results are already here. They're not just outcomes; they're signals. They reflect your clarity, your character, and your consistency. The question is, Are you willing to listen, and adjust based on what they're revealing?

James C. Collins, the author of several best-selling business books, including *Good to Great*, after years of researching business success and leadership, concludes:

> In the end, it is impossible to have a great life unless it is a meaningful life. And it is very difficult to have a meaningful life without meaningful work. Perhaps, then, you might gain that rare tranquility that comes from knowing that you've had a hand in creating something of intrinsic excellence that makes a contribution. Indeed, you might even gain that deepest of all satisfactions: knowing that your short time here on this earth has been well spent, and that it mattered.[54]

Are you like me? At the end of your life, is what you want to hear, "Well done, good and faithful servant"?

A GRADUAL DAWNING

I make it a habit to start each day by reflecting on what I'm grateful for. The list is long now and still growing, but it wasn't always like this. Gratitude didn't come naturally to me; it wasn't my default setting. It was something I had to learn and, more importantly, something I got to practice.

Now it's the cornerstone of my mornings. It sets the tone, centers my spirit, and brings me back to what matters most. Before the demands of the day can crowd in, before emails, meetings, or distractions start pulling me in every direction, I anchor myself in thankfulness. Gratitude reminds me of what I have, not what I lack. It shifts my focus from scarcity to abundance, from stress to peace, from self-criticism to grace.

This daily pause to name what I'm thankful for has rewired how I think. It's made me more grounded, more resilient, more joyful, and more aware of how much is already working in my life. Gratitude doesn't make the hard things go away, but it gives me strength to face them without being consumed by them.

"I never lose. I either win or learn."
NELSON MANDELA

For much of my life, though, I was consumed by lesser things, distractions that looked like ambition but weren't rooted in anything real. I remember a season when I was fixated on fitness magazines. At the time, I weighed 235 pounds and spent way too much mental energy comparing myself to the lean, sculpted, airbrushed men gracing every cover, guys in their midtwenties with chiseled abs, perfect hair, and flawless smiles.

One day I found myself staring at one of those covers, and I started laughing.

Until that moment, I had believed the quiet, persistent lie: "You could still be that guy." But suddenly, something in me shifted. I saw that image for what it was: not a standard but a distraction. I realized that ideal was never mine. It was a socially conditioned illusion I had unconsciously adopted. And I had been measuring myself against it for far too long.

That voice wasn't rooted in gratitude. It was rooted in comparison, insecurity, and self-judgment.

The truth is, I never really wanted to be that guy. What I do want is to be healthy, be strong, be grounded, be able to move freely, live actively, and feel good in my own skin. But because I wasn't doing what it would take to look like a fitness model, I had convinced myself it wasn't worth trying at all. "If I can't look like that, why bother going to the gym?" I thought.

That's the trap. Comparison kills commitment. And ingratitude is what feeds the comparison.

Gratitude, on the other hand, grounds me in what is real and lasting. It reminds me of what I've been given, what I'm capable of, and who I'm becoming.

That's why I start every day with it. It's not fluff. It's not a motivational slogan. It's the foundation for everything else.

One of the biggest by-products of pursuing a clear vision is that it reveals where we've chased the wrong things for far too long. I still wanted to be fit, but my why had to change. That morning, I finally let go of competing with the glossy cover models (as ridiculous as that sounds), and I exchanged it for a vision that was far more meaningful: being healthy enough to play with my grandchildren and great-grandchildren someday. I wanted to lower my risk for disease, take adventurous trips, and have the energy to fully enjoy my life.

Interestingly, my obsession with those magazines had at least one by-product: I developed the habit of going to the gym and running. It helped my body, but it didn't help my soul, because it wasn't connected to a deeper purpose. It didn't empower me. It just reminded me I wasn't enough.

But that morning, that moment of unexpected laughter, was a breakthrough. I didn't shame myself for having chased the wrong ideal. I celebrated the clarity. I've learned that if we're growing, we're learning. And when we're learning, we'll inevitably discover blind spots, flaws, and false beliefs we didn't see before.

That's not a reason to feel shame. That's a reason to celebrate. Insight is a gift. It corrects our course, and even more importantly, it softens our hearts.

Every insight gives us a choice: We can stay stuck in old patterns, or we can move forward with new wisdom. That choice is one of life's greatest gifts.

And gratitude is what helps us recognize it.

Insights are like a genie coming out of a bottle. Once you look them in the eye, you can't stuff them back in. We can still make excuses, point fingers, and blame circumstances, but deep down we know the truth. If we've blamed our spouse for being a great cook and that's why we're overweight, we can't hide any longer the fact that we've chosen to eat too much. If we have a problem with gambling, alcohol, drugs, or shopping, and our parents modeled that behavior, we now realize we, as mature adults, get to own our choices and live responsibly. If we've excused our poor behavior at home with our spouse and kids because we're tired when we get home each day, we recognize the painful results of our previous excuses and choose to be fully present, attentive, and kind. Remember that how people feel around you is affected more by who you are than by what you say. Let those you love feel your joy in them. If they don't feel your love, even your wisest (and most often repeated) words become just background noise. As 1 Corinthians 13:1

says, "If I could speak all the languages of earth and of angels, but didn't love others, I would only be a noisy gong or a clanging cymbal" (NLT).

Some insights come with a laugh, like my fixation on having the perfect body. Others are far less funny. I spent years building an elaborate justification for my behaviors around dating, drinking, and gambling, telling myself that I deserved to unwind, to indulge, to disengage. I told myself I was doing enough in other areas of my life, so I didn't need to change the ones that were hurting the people closest to me. That self-serving logic worked for a while, until I saw it clearly for what it was: a way to avoid responsibility, a way to stay stuck in my predictable past.

That moment of clarity put me at a crossroads: Would I walk toward truth, growth, and restored relationships, or would I double down on defensiveness and cling to the illusion of being right?

That's the decision we all face when the light bulb flickers on. We get to choose: honesty or self-deception, growth or stagnation, humility or pride?

And in a culture obsessed with perfection and performance, it's even harder to admit when we're wrong or flawed in any way. That said, I'm not advocating for morbid introspection. We're not called to scour the depths of our souls looking for shame. Beating ourselves up with guilt or wallowing in regret won't lead to change. Rigorous honesty, however, grounded in the truth that we are already loved, accepted, and treasured by God—that's the path that leads to freedom. That's what produces the joy of transformation, not the burden of shame.

Curiosity and self-discovery are the fertilizer for The Results Tree. Writing this book has given me a front-row seat to the process of looking inward and reflecting on a lifetime of lessons learned and lessons still to come. I've asked myself tough questions: Is this belief still serving me?

Where did it come from? Does it align with who I truly am and who I want to become? And now that I'm on a better path, will I stay the course? Will I protect the vision I've committed to, or let my past write too much of my future?

At every moment, you and I have a choice

> » to take responsibility and seek solutions, or insist on being right;
> » to tell the truth, or shade it to look better or escape discomfort;
> » to bring healing, or hurt the people we love;
> » to pursue emotional health, or hide behind self-deception;
> » to care about others, or use them for personal gain.

That's a humbling checklist. But it's a helpful one too. It helps me evaluate not just my actions but my intentions and results. It helps me stay grounded in who I am committed to be.

Results in Relationships

You and I are masters of disguise. We all know how to wear masks, change our voices, and say whatever it takes to impress people or avoid exposure. It's part of being human. I'm not suggesting we should walk up to everyone we meet and share our deepest secrets, but every one of us needs at least one person who is a true confidant. Every human heart longs to be fully known and deeply loved, and one without the other won't do.

The problem is most of us are terrified of lowering our masks. We fear the people in front of us will either weaponize what they learn or run away laughing. I'm not sure which is worse. Many of us have trusted the wrong people before, only to have our vulnerability used against us. It makes us cautious, even gun-shy. Don't give up. Find someone safe. It may be a close friend, a wise mentor, or even a counselor or coach you've hired. However it comes, make sure you have that person in your life.

"Candor is a compliment; it implies equality. It's how true friends talk."
PEGGY NOONAN

Remember, results in relationships aren't always the same. When you act with kindness and integrity, you'll build stronger connections with most people, but not with everyone. You can't make an alcoholic stop lying. You can't make an abuser suddenly treat you with honor. You can only be responsible for your part. You can offer a path forward, and the other person gets to choose it. If the damage is severe and there's no sign of repentance, wisdom means protecting yourself. Love doesn't mean staying in harm's way. Love also means drawing boundaries strong enough to protect the life God entrusted to you. Dr. Anne Brown comments, "Toxic people create chaos, point fingers, shift blame, and avoid taking responsibility."[55] Do you have someone in your life who fits this description? A wise but unknown person observed, "A toxic person only changes their victims, never themselves."[56]

As I mentioned earlier, when I met Kristie, I wanted to present myself as a great catch. Lying would have been easy and convenient, but as the relationship progressed, I knew I had to tell her about my past. If she chose to walk away, so be it, but I wasn't willing to base our relationship on a lie. The result of finding the courage to speak the truth strengthened our connection. She may have been shocked (I would have been), but she appreciated my being honest with her.

For my entire life, I've tried to come across as completely cool and confident, but underneath the mask I was terrified of conflict. A counselor once shared that in tense communication, people either "get big" (sit up, glare, raise their voices, make demands) or "get little" (slink in the chair, avoid eye contact, mumble, and give in to the demands). That may be true for most people, but I had another reaction: I was sure I was going to turn into a pillar of salt or spontaneously combust! Marriage has taught me to face my fears, become a much better listener, and take 100 percent responsibility.

Marriage can be the source of the greatest joy or the deepest heartache. The term *soulmate* describes our hope that this relationship will complete us. And despite the statistics about domestic abuse and divorce, a good marriage is our best emotional investment. A study by the University of Chicago found that married people are 30 percent happier than those who are single.[57] Similarly, economists Shawn Grover and John Helliwell report that marriage predicts happiness better than income, education, and job satisfaction.[58] In other words, a good marriage takes work, but it has exponential benefits of joy, peace, meaning, and connectedness.

But there's another graduate school I've attended: parenting. When COVID caused lockdowns, I and a few billion other people on the planet worked from home. As everyone knows, there were benefits to this arrangement: no commute and easy access to the refrigerator, among others. But there were problems. My dear children, Preston, MG, and Harrison, were also at home all day every day, and they didn't read the manual on home office etiquette. The interruptions triggered me, and patient requests soon turned into barking demands. After the twentieth time that I told them to be quiet and stay out of my office, I shared my frustrations with my friend Rome. I thought he would commiserate with me. Wrong. He said,

"Gabriel, what if your kids are there to trigger you, to show you what you need to work on, to teach you patience and self-control?" I groaned. I didn't want to hear it, but he wasn't finished. "Yes, I know you have professional coaches to speak into your life, but your kids are the best coaches you could find. They're relentless, and they're free!"

Intangibles are hard to measure, but they're incredibly important. In their outstanding book *The Leadership Challenge*, James Kouzes and Barry Posner observe, "Leadership is not an affair of the head. Leadership is an affair of the heart." They make this startling claim: "Of all the things that sustain a leader over time, love is the most lasting. The best-kept secret of successful leaders is love: staying in love with leading, with the people who do the work, with what their organizations produce, and with those who honor the organization by using its work."[59]

"People do not decide their futures, they decide their habits and their habits decide their futures."

F. M. ALEXANDER

CONSTANT RENEGOTIATION

The concepts of The Results Tree enable us to be present with our intentions, acknowledge our progress, and make any necessary corrections. I may set a goal and make real progress to achieve it but then realize it doesn't quite fit with my vision. Or a continually clarified vision sometimes prompts me to adjust my goals. My career as a navigator gives me a perfect illustration. Imagine a string pulled tight between two cities. When the plane is put on autopilot, the navigation system constantly makes minute adjustments—left, right, up, or down—to stay as close as possible to the thread. The air between destinations isn't static. It's continually changing as the plane flies through weather fronts and over mountains, and as winds and temperatures change. The temperature may seem insignificant, but when it changes, the density of the air is affected, which alters how air passes over the wings. In the same way, our vision is our thread, but changing conditions call us to make continual midcourse corrections to stay on the right path. We're constantly adjusting our efforts to address realities in our current environment and recommitting to the steps to reach our goals. The need to make adjustments isn't because there's something wrong with us; instead, it shows that we live in a dynamic world, so we need to be observant and wise.

Sometimes the changes are small and take time to implement, but occasionally we need to make quick decisions. As you recall, in the leadership program I described, we did a powerful exercise where we leaned out over a one-hundred-foot cliff to test our willingness to risk and trust. In the same program we did another exercise where we started at the bottom of the same cliff and climbed to the top. Again, we had climbing harnesses and climbing shoes and were top-roped and on belay to keep us from falling. Most participants were inexperienced and cautious, but one of the guys was a skilled climber. This guy took huge leaps from one hand-hold to another. I was the instructor, right under him, and I'd never seen anything like it! At one point he jumped from a crevasse to a diamond-shaped rock about the size of a coffee table sticking out from the face of the cliff about eighty feet up. His next move was to launch himself to another rock jutting out of the cliff. He curled his body to make himself into a spring, and with all his might he launched his body up and over, but the force of his jump dislodged the rock he was standing on! Gravity, I noticed immediately, waits for no one. I'm glad I was paying attention because I had only about a second to respond. For some unknown reason I chose to get skinny and press myself into a tiny gap in front of me. A ton of falling stone crashed just behind me. If I'd stepped back, it would have crushed me. If I'd stayed still, it would have crushed me. My snap decision, and the only one to save my life, was to step forward into the gap.

The guy holding the rope tried to jump out of the way, but a piece of rock hit him in the shin. The spotter was quick enough to sidestep the shattered, flying pieces, and the guy on the cliff was dangling with a bird's-eye view of the chaotic scene below. When the rock dislodged, it hit his foot and crushed one of his toes. We lowered him to the ground, carried him about a mile out of the canyon, and drove him an hour to the emergency room.

The next morning, I went back to the bottom of the cliff. I stood where I'd been the previous day. I looked up, then stared at the small gap in the rock where I'd pressed my body and noticed the debris from the fallen rock behind me. Some of the rock had shattered, but a large part was intact, smashed into the ground, leaning at an angle. I kicked at it, felt it with my hands, and imagined what would have happened if I hadn't moved in the right way at the right time. Grateful? Yeah, beyond grateful. Amazed and grateful. It didn't take long to draw a lesson from the experience. I hadn't run away from the risk. I moved forward, and I was alive that morning because I'd made that choice. Lest you think that's a contrived lesson, the buffalo, American bison, use the same principle. They "turn into a snowstorm rather than drifting with the wind because they instinctively know that walking into the storm will get them out of the weather quicker."[60] If we try to avoid trouble, the solution will be delayed, it will probably get worse, and we will have established an unhealthy pattern. Be a bison. Move toward life's storms. As I mentioned before, the shortest distance is through.

In curiosity I stepped up on top of the rock. In an instant I realized it wasn't steady. The point of it was in the earth, but it tipped over. I put more weight on the edge that had just rocked up and balanced it. It then tipped the other way. After going back and forth, like a teeter-totter, I noticed the bottom angle of the rock was burying more deeply into the earth and becoming more stable. This illustrates the second lesson from that experience, which is that traumatic events can rock us, but if we expend energy in the right way, we'll become more secure and stable. I also realized that the normal concept of balance is a lie. Plenty of people talk about finding that perfect place of work-life balance, but it never happens. Instead, we need to use our attention and energy to rock our lives back and forth, finding stability as we accept it tipping one way and then the other. We focus on one priority (or several) at a time, and then we give time and attention to another one. We find a real sense of balance as we address our ever-shifting circumstances with wisdom, strength, and courage. Here's the point: Find and stay as close to the center as possible, layering one good and godly choice on top of another.

Passion and Reason

Some of us need to be honest: We refuse to accept anything less than perfection, and we drive ourselves and others crazy trying to get there. That produces frustration, resentment, and exhaustion. Is perfection worth it? Is it even possible, or is it a fool's errand? At a national convention Pastor Craig Groeschel introduced the concept of GETMO, which means "good enough to move on." He's not advocating mediocrity; he's recommending reason. Leaders and other creative people like to think outside the box, but you can't do that in every area, or you'll die from mental fatigue. He suggests we "think inside the box" most of the time. This creates constraints, but that's not a bad thing.

Don't let your passion for perfection become a hindrance to your results. It's wonderful to be known for excellence, but zeal needs to be tempered by reason. If you're not sure where the blend and balance can be found, talk to your coach, mentor, or some other leader who can help you. Leadership expert Tom Peters comments, "Excellent firms don't believe in excellence—only in constant improvement and constant change."[61] Similarly, in the Air Force we often said, "Don't let perfection be the enemy of the good."

Connect to Your Vision Every Day

Today, my vision is so real, so immediate, and so present that I don't have to set aside time in my day to think about it. It has become the very fabric of my life. It's continually present, a vital part of me. That wasn't the case when The Results Tree first crystallized. When you start, you need visible reminders: Put your vision and a few goals on a note on your bathroom mirror, post a meaningful poem on the bulletin board, write your vision on an index card and put it in your wallet or purse, make your vision statement your computer's wallpaper, make a poster and frame it, and so on. You might buy a package of gold stars to remind you of a particular goal, such as losing ten pounds in the next thirteen weeks. Put a star on the handle of the refrigerator, on the cabinet where you keep snacks, on the bathroom scale, on your computer at the office to remind you when someone brings donuts, and where you look at yourself in the mirror. Whatever works for you, create a touchstone. The point is to use any reminder you need to keep goals in front of you. If you need to staple your vision to your forehead, do it! These reminders trigger you in the present moment back to your higher motivations and goals so you have a clear choice to follow through or not. In this way you interrupt what's been automatic, and you're crafting new, healthier habits. You might use different reminders depending on the domain. For instance, the way to keep your financial goal in plain sight might be different from goals about your fitness, faith, friendships, or mental focus.

And here's another trick: Talk about it. No, don't bore people to death by talking incessantly about it, but at least once a day, find somebody to talk about what's motivating you to be and do your best. Ask them to tell their stories of passion and purpose, and listen well. You might learn something!

Let's go back to the beginning: Your results demonstrate your actual vision for your life. If your results show debt, poor health, or strained relationships, the sobering truth is that is what you've created. Let that sink in. Or perhaps you're financially solid, outwardly successful, and even healthy, yet still restless, sensing something is missing. That too is the fruit of actions, and the emptiness is that it's not yet rooted in vision. The life you live today is the one shaped by the beliefs, choices, and patterns you've allowed. When your results don't align with your stated vision, it is often the signal of an unresolved limiting belief quietly running the show. This is not condemnation; it is revelation. You've simply located the next place where healing, alignment, and growth can occur. Sometimes that takes deeper reflection, and in certain cases, the help of trusted guides or professionals to uncover what has been buried.

This realization may feel heavy at first, but in truth it is profoundly freeing. It proves that The Results Tree works with perfect clarity. It reflects what you have been sowing, whether consciously or unconsciously. Results show up in every area of life: Some are easy to measure, like numbers on a scale or in a bank account, while others, such as peace, love, respect, and joy, defy simple metrics but are infinitely more valuable. SMART goals have their place, but some of the most important fruit grows beyond charts and checklists. Measurable is nice, but love is nicer. For Kristie and me, the sweetest results are not business wins but watching our children grow into kind, respectful, and joyful people. Their laughter, their resilience, even their challenges remind us daily that what we sow matters, and they push us to keep becoming our best selves.

So pay attention. Be observant with your results, not with pride or shame, but with curiosity. Treat them as feedback, not verdicts. The encouraging ones remind you to give thanks and stay the course. The disappointing ones are invitations to look deeper, to learn, to realign. Like fruit on a tree, results ripen in season. They may take time, but they always reveal the seeds you've planted through vision, intention, and action. This is the promise of The Results Tree: You are always creating results, and you always have the power to begin again. The question before you is simple and profound: From this moment forward, what kind of fruit will you choose to grow?

> I'd love to walk with you on this journey. Check out The Results Tree Experience eCourse, where I'll guide you step-by-step as you put this framework into practice and move from insight to action.

Chapter 7

ENJOY THE JOURNEY!

Nothing is more fulfilling and satisfying than knowing what God has designed us for. We could be great in our careers, but that does not mean we have fulfilled what our Creator made us to be. Real success starts with discovering God's purpose and taking action toward it. The road to fulfilling His purpose will be full of struggles and sacrifices, but it will always be worth it.

RICK WARREN

Results matter, but your identity is most important. The fruits of your efforts, the results you see in every area of life, don't define you. Instead, the results are feedback that can always be traced back to your vision. If you have put your faith in Jesus, you are deeply loved, completely forgiven, and totally accepted because you are "in Christ." Paul uses this shorthand phrase dozens of times in his letters. You are in Christ in His death on the cross, so His complete payment for sin has been applied to you. You are in Christ in His resurrection, so you share His supernatural life. You are in Christ in His ascension to heaven's throne, so you also are royalty. It just doesn't get any better than that! No amount of fame, wealth, knowledge, or pleasure can compare.

What matters is your impact on people, the description of your life in your obituary, and the legacy you leave for those you love. When we look at a decorated Christmas tree, the bright and shiny ornaments are attractive, but what matters more is the giving and receiving of love and the deeper meaning of the season—that Almighty God lowered Himself to become one of us to pay the price for sin we should have paid and live the life we couldn't live. Christmas means far more than unwrapping presents and eating too much. Your results are ornaments. They remind you of a deeper meaning. They are a reflection of where you've been investing your time, talent, and treasure.

"Among the things you can give and still keep are your word, a smile, and a grateful heart."

ZIG ZIGLAR

Kristie and I have friends, Nora and Jack, who have a tragic yet heartwarming story. Jack was diagnosed with cancer and endured chemo and radiation. During this painful time, Nora told me that there was always one of their kids' cars in the driveway. They loved and honored their dad, and they were incredibly supportive of their mom. Day after day, when Jack and Nora struggled with physical and emotional exhaustion, their children spoke loudly without saying a word, "I see you. I love you. You can count on me." Their presence says more about the legacy of Nora and Jack than anything else I can imagine.

Before I was born, during their first years of marriage my parents didn't have much. Like many young couples starting out, they were short on money but full of love and determination to create a meaningful life together. Their first Christmases were simple, no fancy decorations, no curated tree, just creativity, heart, and whatever they had on hand.

One year they decided to make their own ornaments. With yarn, felt scraps, and imagination, they sat together and crafted the "Twelve Days of Christmas"—lords, maids, drummers, dancers—and mixed in some snowmen, reindeer, and whatever else came to mind. Some of them didn't quite look like what they were supposed to, but that wasn't the point. What mattered was the time spent together, the laughter, and the joy of creating something from nothing.

As I grew up, those same handmade ornaments came out every December. They became part of our family's Christmas tradition. Each year, we hung them on the tree, and I learned that Christmas didn't need to be perfect to be meaningful.

Later, when our family became a bit more financially secure, my mom started collecting more polished, store-bought ornaments, usually scooped up after Christmas at 90 percent off. Over time the handmade ones made fewer appearances on the tree, but they were never thrown away. They live in a box in the attic, and every year when we decorate, we open it and smile. Sometimes one or two of those frayed little ornaments still make it onto the tree for nostalgia's sake and as a quiet tribute to those early years, when love, not money, made the season bright.

Like our cherished ornaments, the results of our accomplished goals may last for only a season. We reach our target weight, we've saved enough for retirement, we've written the book we've thought about for so long, and now it's time to move to a new goal. Of course, relationship goals aren't discarded. They remain. They change as children grow and mature, so we don't treat young adults the way we treated them when they were in elementary school. They grow, and if we're wise, we grow right along with them. The fruit of our love when they're five is very different from the fruit of our love when they have children and invite us to pour love into them. The fruit of the past doesn't become irrelevant; each positive result is a signpost of progress on the journey. We've done it before, and we have confidence we can tackle new goals.

Start Where You Are

Sure, it's thrilling to tell people that your dream is to climb Mount Everest, but if you're carrying a few too many pounds and are out of shape, your goal should be putting your shoes on and walking around the neighborhood. In *Atomic Habits*, James Clear has terrific advice. For instance:

> All big things come from small beginnings. The seed of every habit is a single, tiny decision. But as that decision is repeated, a habit sprouts and grows stronger. Roots entrench themselves and branches grow. The task of breaking a bad habit is like uprooting a powerful oak within us. And the task of building a good habit is like cultivating a delicate flower one day at a time.

He writes that every decision is part of a habit, for good or ill:

> Every action you take is a vote for the type of person you wish to become. No single instance will transform your beliefs, but as the votes build up, so does the evidence of your new identity. This is one reason why meaningful change does not require radical change. Small habits can make a meaningful difference by providing evidence of a

new identity. And if a change is meaningful, it is actually big. That's the paradox of making small improvements.⁶²

When I talk to someone who dares to pursue a vision through thick and thin, I get emotional because I see such beauty and power in that person. God has given us incredible opportunities to thrive. We start at different places and with different resources, but He has given us one thing in common: today, right now, this minute—that's the present. What we do with it makes a world of difference, not only to us but more particularly to those around us.

I believe God withholds some blessings because He knows we can't handle them. We're too self-absorbed, so greater success would reinforce this flaw. And sometimes it's a disaster. Many of us dream about winning the lottery as a shortcut to getting everything we've ever wanted. However, an article about these winners gives a more sobering perspective:

> Most lottery dreams share a few common themes: yachts and lobster tails, big tips, fast cars, the fast life and a mansion for mom. In reality, instant entry to the nouveau riche class has a way of wrecking friendships, destroying marriages, ending in bankruptcy or worse. Winning the lottery might seem like a dream come true, but mountains of unearned money are irresistible to greedy and resentful friends and relatives, con artists and charity cases, who scurry out of the woodwork to grab as much of it as they can. In other cases, it's the lottery winners themselves who can't get out of their own way—reckless spending, giving, partying and gambling leave some worse off than they started.⁶³

Pastor Rick Warren cuts through any unrealistic expectations of an easy life: "Before every blessing, there is a testing. God tests you with stress before he trusts you with success. These are the principles of persistent prayer. God is going to test you before he blesses you."⁶⁴

Do you want a fulfilling, meaningful, happy life? Don't look for shortcuts. Our task (one we've addressed many times in this book) is to uncover our hidden passion to make a positive impact and pursue it with all our hearts. Will there be some selfish motives mixed in? Absolutely. We won't have pure motives until our transformation when we see Jesus face-to-face, but God has a way of exposing our selfishness. Then we have another choice: Confess it and embrace the forgiveness God has already poured out in Jesus, or make excuses and keep our hearts focused on secondary things such as power, wealth, pleasure, and approval. Again, don't get me wrong. There's nothing in the world wrong with power, wealth, pleasure, and approval if they're gifts from a gracious God instead of our hearts' primary focus. Jesus warned that something will have priority in our hearts, and He's the One who deserves that place: "No one can serve two masters. Either you will hate the one and love the other, or you will be devoted to the one and despise the other. You cannot serve both God and money [or anything else]" (Matt. 6:24).

"The best way to find yourself is to lose yourself in the service of others."
MAHATMA GANDHI

Hard times test us and strengthen us, if we'll let them. Not long after Kristie and I got married, we hit a brick wall in our finances. Our two parked cars had been wrecked by a drunk driver, the pipes burst and flooded our house, and we didn't have enough money to pay utility bills and taxes. These results were very real and devastating. It was a come-to-Jesus moment. Kristie had health problems; I worried about everything. We had to stop and dig deep to redefine and reengage with our purpose. But from that painful experience came something truly valuable:

We learned that when we both committed ourselves to the same vision and goals, we could overcome any obstacles.

Years ago I ran for a state senate seat in California. It seemed like a logical extension of my time in uniform. I was sure I could do a great job in office. I loved the campaign because it called attention to all my best qualities, but I also had to defend myself from those who weren't exactly enamored with my greatness. I lost the race. I was heartbroken and suffered depression for a time. When I look back, I'm pretty sure winning that election would have destroyed our marriage, I would have neglected our children, and I would have missed the amazing life I live now. God spared me from political victory. Garth Brooks captured the lesson I learned from this experience in his song "Unanswered Prayers": Sometimes when God doesn't grant us what we pray for, it's actually a blessing in disguise.[65]

Types of Trees

Throughout this book you've probably identified the kind of tree you are today, the kinds around you, and the kind you want to become. Let's look at these:

Saplings

Some people reading this book don't have mighty oaks with abundant results, yet they are saplings, and they're eager to see some big fruit on the branches (for oaks, the fruit is acorns). Surely you remember the short film *A Charlie Brown Christmas*. What happened when he put the big star on the top of the tree? It bent over because it wasn't strong enough to hold it. Be realistic about the time growth will take, and celebrate every step forward and every evidence of fruit.

Some of us aren't saplings yet. We're seeds. Don't be distressed; we all start there! Plant in yourself the seed of a vision that captures your imagination. When that seed sprouts, the first thing that happens is that a root goes deep into the soil. Give your vision the nourishment it needs in the early months and years. Then, the shoot rises above the ground, forming a stem. Soon, leaves and branches begin to form. If that's where you are today, that's fantastic! You'll have visible results soon enough, and you'll be encouraged to keep growing. The worst thing you can do to a sprouting seed is dig it up again and again to see why it isn't growing faster. Every gardener is a person of faith. The seed looks inert, lifeless, and small, but planted in the right soil with water and sunlight, the amazing process of growth happens. If your vision is only a seed, have faith that planting and nourishing it will produce something wonderful, in time. When you don't see much happening, call on your faith, grit, determination, and tenacity to keep doing the things that promise growth and eventually a great harvest of fruit. There's absolutely nothing wrong with a sapling. It's right where it should be in the developmental process.

"A life is not important except in the impact it has on other lives."
JACKIE ROBINSON

Trees aren't jealous of other trees. An apple tree isn't angry that it can't produce pecans. And trees can't change their environment, but we can. We can make better choices about the five people who have the most influence on us (either to affirm them, change them, or replace them); we can choose how we spend our time; we can choose the books, music, and podcasts that fill our minds; we can choose to go to a small-group Bible study instead of the bar; we can choose to take an extra couple of minutes to make a healthy lunch instead of grabbing another burger and fries; we can choose to put that money into an IRA instead of buying the latest gadget... You get the idea.

Wherever we are on the journey, we need milestones ("inchstones" if a mile is too far) to show us that we're making progress, not so far that we get tired and discouraged and not so easy that we lose motivation. Especially at the beginning of using The Results Tree, setting and reaching clear goals goes a long way to developing healthy habits and encouraging you to trust that this process works.

Withered Trees

Those we identified in the first chapter as stuck or discouraged are like fruit trees in a prolonged drought. They have the shape of a tree, but there's very little fruit, and the branches are brittle. The causes may be varied: a toxic relationship that saps your energy and hope, a failure you can't seem to get over, a bitter disappointment that someone you trusted let you down, an unexpected and unwanted diagnosis, or something else entirely. Staring at the barren branches doesn't help things. Attention needs to go to the roots and the soil. What's the environment of the root system? Obviously, it's not fertile enough to nourish a vision. Does it need water and fertilizer, or would it be better to replant it in a better place with more or less sunlight?

What excuses have you used for avoiding hard decisions, perhaps some of them excruciatingly hard? Every problem is a test, not to punish you for being deficient but to give you an opportunity to grow stronger and wiser. Don't settle for staying stuck. Find a mentor, coach, or counselor who can help you take steps forward to find more nourishment for your roots. Bringing a dying plant back to life requires much more effort than tending it well while it's healthy, but you have to start where you are today and make the best of it. Plenty of people have been where you are and turned their lives into exactly what they really want. You can too!

We want to avoid a victim mentality, but the truth is that some of us really are victims. What's the difference? A victim mentality is a coping strategy to avoid responsibility and making tough decisions. No matter how much people try to help them, victims self-sabotage. Remaining stuck feels better than mustering the courage to move forward. True victims of all kinds of abuse, abandonment, and betrayal have suffered deep wounds that need to be healed. Their tree is withered, not because they made bad decisions and had wrong priorities, but because someone poured poison on their root system. They need love, support, and practical assistance to reclaim their lives and grow strong again.

Lots of Disconnected Fruit

I don't have to look very far for an example of someone who looked very successful but felt confused and empty. I was an example of this person. I accomplished a lot and met a lot of goals, but my roots weren't in the right soil. My intention was self-focused, not others-focused. Achievement motivated me for a while, but eventually it wasn't enough. How many rungs on the ladder did I need to climb to feel fulfilled? It was always one more.

Simon Sinek observes, "Work ethic is giving great effort to complete a task. Passion is giving great effort to advance a cause."[66] I had a sterling work ethic, and I was skilled at setting SMART goals, but I was focused on the task, not a greater cause. Earlier I told the story of being on the top of a cliff with my friend Michael and admitting that I was overweight at 235 pounds. I set a goal of getting under 200, and I came very close to it at 204.

The benefits of feeling better, having amazing sex, lowering my heart risk, and being healthy enough to play one day with my great-grandchildren were there, but they came into clearer focus later. During the months from September on the cliff to March, when COVID locked down the gyms, I was focused primarily on proving I could reach the goal. It was all about me. As my greater cause wasn't clear, COVID gave me plenty of excuses to give up, eat more, and exercise less. My why wasn't big enough.

A couple of years later Kristie and I had a revelation of the importance of letting our vision determine our destiny. I had been driven to succeed, comparing myself with others, proud when I surpassed them and angry when I didn't. I thought that was just the way life worked. I was wrong. We took a long, hard look at our lives, humbled ourselves to admit we'd been self-focused, and began to sink our roots into a vision that's far bigger than our comfort, pleasure, and stuff. Our perspective of our legacy, our tombstone test, galvanized our thoughts and plans. We wanted to leave our children with more than cars, houses, and investment accounts; we wanted to leave them a tradition of love, laughter, gratitude, compassion, and wisdom.

I voiced that vision years before, but I didn't own it. It wasn't at the top of my mind. It didn't consume my thoughts or stir my imagination. Now it did. I had a why to give substance and direction to my what and my how.

Plenty of people have a boatload of knowledge, but few have the scarce commodity of wisdom. We can gain wisdom in several different ways: We can gain insights from reading books and listening to speakers and then internalizing and applying the concepts; we can learn by watching the mistakes of others and realizing we don't want to fall into the same holes; or we can learn the hard way, from our own mistakes. For any of these we need an open mind and a pliable heart, a willingness to admit we're wrong or shortsighted, and the courage to try something new. It's my choice which path to take. And it's your choice.

An Oak

Imagine a mature, sturdy oak. These are often the biggest and strongest trees in a forest. Animals live in the branches and under the canopy. Oaks reach this point through many years of steady growth, in storms and in sunshine, drought and rain. You may be like an oak. Perhaps you've carved out a space in life's forest with a bold vision, clear intentions to reach specific goals, and committed action, and you've achieved amazing results. Along the way you've weathered your share of storms, and you may have lost a few limbs, but you learned important lessons from each experience.

I have three pieces of advice for you. First, celebrate. Stop often to consider the ups and downs, the twists and turns of your journey, and be thankful for the path, the people who have helped you succeed, and the lessons you've learned. Second, be a mentor. Pour yourself into the next generation. Wisdom isn't just acquired through personal trial and error; those you mentor can learn from *your* trials and errors! And third, keep dreaming, keep reaching, keep engaging your creativity and passion to make a difference. Until you're in the ground, you have a lot to offer.

Richard Branson, the founder of Virgin Group, remembers the best advice he ever received: "If you asked every person in the world who gave them their best advice, it is a safe bet that most would say it was their mother. I am no exception. My mother has taught me many valuable lessons that have helped shape my life. But *having no regrets* stands out above all others because it has informed every aspect of my life and every business decision we have ever made."[67] Those who follow the principles and practices of The Results Tree can live a life without regrets.

REPLACE YOURSELF

I've heard parents of grown children say that their greatest joy is seeing their kids become wonderful parents to their kids. They trained their replacements in their genealogical tree. We normally think of training replacements in more structured environments, such as business or the military. Insecure leaders don't train people to take their place for any number of reasons: They may tell themselves they're immortal and will never fade away; they may conclude no one is capable of replacing them; or, more likely, they would feel threatened if someone were to take their place and do a better job. Whatever the reason, the failure to pour time and resources into those who come behind us is a leadership flaw. The best leaders equip those at every level to think, plan, and provide resources to raise competent leaders throughout the organization. In one way that's their main job, no matter what their business card says. Helping people understand how the larger organization operates, and their place in it, adds value and raises the motivation level because they see that what they do matters.

At one point in my military career I was an air adviser to air forces in countries of Central and South America. I soon noticed that the many of the airmen we were deployed to train didn't have a commitment to share knowledge with the next generation. Knowledge is power and job security. If no one else knew how to do their job, the airmen believed their jobs were safe. At least that was the theory. Unfortunately, this mindset inhibited the development of people who were (or could have been) rising experts and made organizational improvement next to impossible. There was little or no cross-pollination of ideas. In the US military, when we master a concept or skill, we immediately begin teaching others to be masters. And when we've been a master teacher for a while, we train and evaluate other master teachers to ensure that our instruction, from top to bottom, is accurate, current, and standardized. This culture of training is a major factor in our country's military dominance.

As your journey begins and then accelerates, don't be surprised when others take notice. There will be days when someone asks, "What's different about you?" or, "What are you doing that's working so well?" Take it as a small but powerful confirmation that you are on the right path.

Just remember, to help someone else, you don't need to have it all figured out. You only need to be one step ahead. If the people who ask are aligned with what you're creating and committed to transforming their own lives, this could be the beginning of something even bigger, a power group, a circle of influence, a team that supports one another, holds one another accountable, and speaks the kind of honest feedback that fuels true growth. You were never meant to do this alone. Transformation multiplies when we rise together.

You're Not Getting Out Alive!

How's that for optimism? Actually, a healthy view of our mortality frees us to devote every moment of every day to living on purpose. The process I've described in this book empowers you to be fully present with what matters most. When you realize your time on the planet is a blink in light of eternity, you're motivated for that blink to count long after you're gone. You have a vision of how you can make a difference, and that vision gives you the wisdom to double down on what matters and release what doesn't.

For me, reevaluating every quarter feels just right. It's a rhythm that keeps me honest. Every ninety days, I pause to check my heading, make course corrections, and stay aligned with what matters most. Each stretch of time becomes a window of intentional progress. By setting SMART goals in three meaningful domains every quarter, I finish the year having built momentum across twelve areas of life. Then the next year, I begin again, stronger, clearer, and more grounded.

When this rhythm is multiplied over years, decades, and a lifetime, something extraordinary happens. Your vision becomes reality, not through one massive breakthrough but through the power of consistent, purpose-driven choices. Your vision starts to live in your bones. It shows up in how you speak, lead, love, protect, and invest. It shapes what you give and what you leave behind.

You might be thinking, "That sounds like a lot." And it is. It's not drudgery; it's freedom. The grind only comes when you chase someone else's goals, trying to impress, perform, or survive. That is exhausting. When your goals are born from your vision, when they're rooted in your why, everything changes. You move with clarity. You wake up with purpose. And you discover the joy of living a life that is fully your own.

This isn't about pressure. It's about power, the power to choose, to grow, to build something lasting. That kind of life is anything but a grind. That is the life you were made for.

Rebooting

If you're over twenty-five, you probably remember when computers gave us the dreaded "blue screen of death." Too many programs running, a glitch in the system, and suddenly everything froze. The only way forward was to reboot. Life works the same way. Sometimes we hit an unexpected crash in health, relationships, careers, or finances. When that happens, we need a fresh start.

Kristie is a master at rebooting. She's highly empathetic and deeply spiritual, which means she feels the bumps of life with great intensity. I'm head-forward; she's heart-forward. When she's upset, I've learned to ask one question: "Is it me?" More often than not, it isn't, but even when it is, the way she processes amazes me. She'll step away for fifteen or twenty minutes to wrestle with what is bothering her and return renewed. She doesn't wallow in self-pity, and she doesn't blame others. She owns her part, speaks truth where it's needed, and lets the rest go.

Here's how she puts it:

"As a recovering perfectionist, when something negative happens, my default is to question 'What did I do wrong?' In that moment, I step away to be still. Gabriel calls it rebooting. It takes a few minutes; eventually I emerge with clarity and understanding about what God wants me to do next, and we begin again."

You may not reboot as quickly as Kristie, but the principle is the same. Keep coming back as often as needed. Remind yourself of your identity as a beloved child of God. Use the skills from this book to reset your course and walk forward again.

A Final Word

Congratulations! You've walked through the framework of The Results Tree, and now you know your life is not random. Your results are not accidents. They are mirrors reflecting your vision, clear intention, and committed action. And the miracle is this: You always have the power to begin again. No matter how many false starts, no matter how many setbacks, your next step can put you back on the path of wholeness and purpose.

If you take nothing else from this book, take this: You are not alone on the journey. God has been, is now, and always will be present, inviting you into a life of love, meaning, and courage. Your part is simply to open your heart and, when you falter, to begin again.

As we close, I want to leave you with a prayer from Pastor Groeschel:

> May God bless you with discomfort at easy answers, half-truths, and superficial relationships, so that you may live deep within your heart. May God bless you with anger at injustice, oppression, and exploitation of people, so that you may work for justice, freedom, and peace. May God bless you with tears to shed for those who suffer from pain, rejection, starvation, and war so that you may reach out your hand to comfort them and to turn their pain into joy. And may God bless you with enough foolishness to believe that you can make a difference in this world so that you can do what others claim cannot be done. To bring justice and kindness to all our children and the poor. Amen.[68]

Access free resources, including downloads, worksheets, and guided exercises designed to help you put these principles into practice.

EXERCISE
Becoming an Oak

You've come a long way, through vision, intention, committed action, and now results. And this isn't the finish line. This is where the real-life change begins, not in a single leap but in daily steps, rooted in purpose, moving toward who you're committed to being.

These final questions are designed to help you slow down, reflect deeply, and choose into the long game of transformation.

What are some reasons it's necessary to embrace the process of growth as a gradual journey? What happens when we become too impatient? The Bible says, "Wealth gained hastily will dwindle, but whoever gathers little by little will increase it" (Prov. 13:11, ESV).

_____
_____
_____
_____
_____

Growth that lasts doesn't rush. It roots. Reflect on where you need more grace and patience with yourself.

_____
_____
_____
_____

Whether you feel like a brand-new sapling, a withered tree, an overextended branch, or a strong and steady oak, every stage has purpose, and every tree can grow. What are some intentional steps you will take today, in the next three days, and by next week? Be specific. Make a commitment to yourself.

_____

_____

_____

_____

When setbacks hit, and they always do, what's been your default reaction? How can you learn to reboot and respond in your own way?

_____

_____

_____

_____

You're not the same person who started this journey. You've dug deeper, seen more clearly, and chosen growth, even when it was uncomfortable. Becoming an oak takes time. With each small act of intention, each moment of humility, each choice to reboot instead of retreat, you are becoming stronger, wiser, and more deeply rooted.

Keep going. The world needs what only you can bring. Your vision, when you stay faithful to it, will shape a legacy far beyond what you can imagine today.

You were made for this.

The RESULTS TREE

A Proven Path to the
LIFE YOU *Really* WANT

Appendix A

Uncovering Your Life's Vision

Death has a way of crystallizing our thoughts to help us realize our dreams. Imagine your best friend reading your obituary at your funeral.

To give you an idea of what I'm talking about, let me show you the one I wrote:

> Gabriel James Griess was born in Lincoln, Nebraska, on May 27, 1973, the one and only child of Jim and Polly Griess. Born with jaundice, Gabriel immediately began fighting for life. He was given two blood transfusions at St. Elizabeth Hospital in Lincoln and placed in an incubator. He wasn't aware that he would make the newspaper's front page as the first child placed in the hospital's incubator.
> Gabriel grew up a happy, curious, loving, kind boy who explored the countryside. A few years later he mowed lawns and worked in the fields for Don and Gerry Perry and on the Beckman's farm. When he was just a boy, he set his sights

on becoming governor of Nebraska. His purpose would evolve over the coming years, but the dream of making a difference was present from his childhood. He enjoyed friends, athletics, and academic achievements on his way to graduation and, ultimately, to the Air Force Academy. At the academy, he displayed the grit of "just too dumb to quit," persevered, and graduated in 1995. At the academy and later in flight school in Pensacola and San Antonio, he made some of the most kind, loving, caring, supportive friends a guy could ever know, including Kevin Sellers, Michael Thompson, Mark Holbrook, Ryan Warner, Brad Downs, George Lugo, and many others. In Little Rock he learned to fly the C-130, followed by an assignment in Tokyo and, after 9/11, to combat operations for Afghanistan and Iraq. He eventually was assigned to the Naval Postgraduate School in 2007.

Because of some unexpected twists of fate, or, better yet, the hand of God, Gabriel was introduced to Kristie, the woman who would become his wife, by their mutual friend Lisa Hitchcock. He was in love from the first phone call on October 20, 2008. He and Kristie immediately connected, but both were terrified that they had found their soulmate, or "twin flames," as Kristie likes to call it. Their courtship was quick. Gabriel was assigned to Washington, DC, and was to report in January. Before then he took many trips to Southern California, where Kristie lived, for USC football games and Thanksgiving with her family. On a drive from Los Angeles to DC, somewhere in the desert of New Mexico, Gabriel asked

Kristie, "What would it take for you to go with me to Washington?"

Kristie responded, "When you get your ducks in a row."

Gabriel asked, "Do you mean a sparkly duckie, for your finger?"

She told him, "That's a good place to start!"

Engagement and marriage soon followed. The next few years were a whirlwind. Their son Preston was born, but they lost Gabriel's mom to cancer. Their daughter Mikayla "MG" was born, and then Gabriel's father passed away. The Griess nest was full when Harrison was born and was added to the team.

The Air Force took the family to Northern California, where Gabriel had the opportunity to establish the first-of-its-kind squadron that trained Air Forces from Central and South America. In this role, Gabriel thrived, creatively seeking solutions when budgets, equipment, material, or training were lacking, and seeking to build bridges between communities to overcome communication barriers and build better relationships.

Gabriel then threw his hat in the ring for a political campaign in California that took everything, heart, soul, and finances. The inspiration and the excitement of the race still ripple today but in a different arena. His friend Scott invited him to Dallas to help launch a medical staffing firm, Excel Medical Staffing. This began Gabriel's journey into training, crossing barriers, and building people up. Excel continues to grow and empower those who work in the company, improving how temporary medical clinicians are treated and ultimately helping them grow and be inspired to live their most productive God-given lives. Along the way, he managed to dabble a little bit in real estate, have some fun, and participate in Rotary, Tarrant County College, and local, state, and national politics, all with the desire to have organizations and government serve people well. He was a man on a mission. He connected everything he did to his big, bold vision, and he was tenacious about fulfilling it.

In his final days Gabriel lived a comfortable, joyful, fun life surrounded by his loving wife, Kristie, their three children, nine grandchildren, and four great-grandchildren. It was always his dream to live long enough to hold a great-grandchild, and by the grace of God that happened.

As I look at those of you at his funeral today and see your faces, I know that Gabriel gave a piece of himself to each of you. He often went to a whiteboard, grabbed a spreadsheet or a napkin, and began to break down some challenging problem of yours, dream your dreams with you, and help you put the next few steps in place, steps that have made a difference in your life and, through you, the lives of countless others. His only request of each of you would be to be fully present with those you spend time with, be grateful, stay curious, continue to learn, take risks, live grounded in faith, and create epic experiences. You are his legacy.

I wrote this on a Sunday morning, and by the time I'd finished, I had tears in my eyes. When I read it again, I realized there were no cars, houses, or private jets in my story. My obituary captured the power of what's in my heart. The ability for us to create and participate in our stories is only limited by our curiosity because God, our Creator, is limitless in wisdom, love, kindness, and generosity. He is beyond our imagination, but it's up to us to pursue Him as He pursues us, listen to the voice of the Spirit and His Word in the Scriptures, and exercise faith to take steps toward the vision He gives us.

I live a curious, responsible, intentional life, creating joyful and memorable experiences. That's my why.

Now it's your turn. First, write the obituary you'd like people to read and hear at your funeral. Don't be concerned about punctuation and grammar. Let your mind flow without restraint. Later, you can organize and fine-tune it.

- » Date of death (make it yesterday)
- » List of family
- » The way you lived your life
- » The influence you had on others
- » A summary of why you'll be missed

Try using the Tombstone Test, an AI-guided reflection, to help you craft your own obituary. Seeing the legacy you want to leave brings immediate insight to the choices you're making now and the life you're building in real time.

If you need more room to write, get a journal, a notebook, or sheets of paper. Don't try to rush this exercise. Think deeply and pour out your heart.

Now write an obituary that would be written today with your life *as it is now*, based on how you are living the dreams you've been chasing. How do you know what your dreams are? By how your money and time are being spent and invested. Use the same elements as before.

The Results Tree

Reflect

What are some similarities between your two obituaries?
_____
_____
_____

What are some differences?
_____
_____
_____

What's the impact of this exercise on your commitment to uncovering and articulating your life's vision?
_____
_____
_____

What is one change you will make this week to move your current story closer to your desired one? Circle a date and commit to it.
_____
_____
_____

Appendix B

SMART Goals

Since SMART goals can support your Results Tree journey and help you turn your vision into measurable progress, this appendix provides space to detail your SMART goals and then track each one.

SMART GOAL WORKSHEET

S SPECIFIC	What will be accomplished?
M MEASURABLE	How will you measure success?
A ACHIEVABLE	Do you have the requisite resources and skills?
R RELEVANT	Why is it important? How does the goal align with your vision?
T TIME-BOUND	What is the due date for success?

SMART GOAL TRACKER

	Date/ Time of Goal	Measurable: How will I measure success?	Achievable: My plan on how to achieve the goal, notes on my progress, and revelations from my efforts
WEEK 1			
WEEK 2			
WEEK 3			
WEEK 4			

	Date/ Time of Goal	Measurable: How will I measure success?	Achievable: My plan on how to achieve the goal, notes on my progress, and revelations from my efforts
WEEK 5			
WEEK 6			
WEEK 7			
WEEK 8			
WEEK 9			

	Date/Time of Goal	Measurable: How will I measure success?	Achievable: My plan on how to achieve the goal, notes on my progress, and revelations from my efforts
WEEK 10			
WEEK 11			
WEEK 12			
WEEK 13			

Appendix C

Becoming Self-Aware: A Guided Self-Discovery Exercise

For the want of a nail the shoe was lost.
For the want of a shoe the horse was lost.
For the want of a horse the rider was lost.
For the want of a rider the battle was lost.
For the want of a battle the kingdom was lost.
And all for the want of a horseshoe nail.
George Herbert, 1640

Sometimes the smallest detail, a single nail, can change everything. In the same way, moments, words, or habits from your past may be shaping your present in ways you've never noticed. This exercise is designed to slow you down, help you look inward, and become more aware of what has formed you, how you've responded, and how you want to move forward with clarity and purpose.

Reflection Prompts

Positive shaping

Who or what shaped you in life-giving ways? Think of mentors, moments, or memories that made you stronger, wiser, or more resilient.

_____
_____
_____

Negative shaping

What wounds, failures, or toxic patterns still weigh on you? How have they shaped your behavior or beliefs?

_____
_____
_____

Current priorities

List your five most important people and your five most important priorities. Does your calendar reflect those priorities?

1. _____
2. _____
3. _____
4. _____
5. _____

1. _____
2. _____
3. _____
4. _____
5. _____

Identity and self-concept

Describe yourself in three words that reflect how you actually showed up today (not aspirational). Rate your comfort in your own skin from 0–10. Why did you choose (circle) that score?

Word 1: _____

   1   2   3   4   5   6   7   8   9   10

Word 2: _____

   1   2   3   4   5   6   7   8   9   10

Word 3: _____

   1   2   3   4   5   6   7   8   9   10

Love and loss

Who has loved you most deeply? Whom have you loved the most? How has that giving and receiving shaped you? Recall your happiest and hardest memories. What stories do you tell yourself about them?

_____

_____

_____

Relationships and patterns

List the twenty people you spend the most time with. Score each relationship from 1 (toxic) to 10 (life-giving). What do the patterns reveal?

Person 1: _____
    1 2 3 4 5 6 7 8 9 10

Person 2: _____
    1 2 3 4 5 6 7 8 9 10

Person 3: _____
    1 2 3 4 5 6 7 8 9 10

Person 4: _____
    1 2 3 4 5 6 7 8 9 10

Person 5: _____
    1 2 3 4 5 6 7 8 9 10

Person 6: _____
    1 2 3 4 5 6 7 8 9 10

Person 7: _____
    1 2 3 4 5 6 7 8 9 10

Person 8: _____
    1 2 3 4 5 6 7 8 9 10

Person 9: _____
    1   2   3   4   5   6   7   8   9   10

Person 10: _____
    1   2   3   4   5   6   7   8   9   10

Person 11: _____
    1   2   3   4   5   6   7   8   9   10

Person 12: _____
    1   2   3   4   5   6   7   8   9   10

Person 13: _____
    1   2   3   4   5   6   7   8   9   10

Person 14: _____
    1   2   3   4   5   6   7   8   9   10

Person 15: _____
    1   2   3   4   5   6   7   8   9   10

Person 16: _____
    1   2   3   4   5   6   7   8   9   10

Person 17: _____
    1   2   3   4   5   6   7   8   9   10

Person 18: _____
          1   2   3   4   5   6   7   8   9   10

Person 19: _____
          1   2   3   4   5   6   7   8   9   10

Person 20: _____
          1   2   3   4   5   6   7   8   9   10

From this exercise, consider what conclusions you can draw:

When life gets tough, I _____
_____
_____

When relationships get messy and hard, I _____
_____
_____

My self-concept was shaped by _____
_____
_____

My confidence is at level (0–10) _____ because _____
_____
_____

I have these wounds to address and heal: _____
_____
_____

I get to heal by _____
_____
_____

I've wounded others in these ways: _____
_____
_____

I get to take responsibility for hurting them by _____
_____
_____

I get to apologize for _____
_____
_____

I've tried to cope by doing these things: _____
_____
_____

They worked because _____
_____
_____

They didn't work because _____
_____
_____

Now pause.

What did you learn from this process?
_____
_____
_____

Which past wounds and failures could be reframed as stepping stones?
_____
_____
_____

Why is it important to view every setback as neutral, even useful, rather than catastrophic?
_____
_____
_____

What difference would it make if you simply said, "We'll see," in both your highs and lows?
_____
_____
_____

What difference will this lesson make in your life?
_____
_____
_____

You are not finished; you are becoming. Self-awareness is the seed of transformation. By reflecting honestly on your story, you've chosen clarity over comfort. Keep revisiting what you've uncovered, letting grace and courage guide your next steps. Remember, even the smallest awareness, a single "horseshoe nail," can change everything.

Appendix D

Ten Traits You Can Cultivate

The "10 Things That Require Zero Talent" list has become a popular motivational tool across various platforms, emphasizing traits that individuals can cultivate regardless of innate ability. While its exact origin is unclear, the list has been widely shared and adapted in different contexts.

One notable instance of the list's use is by Bill Gross, the founder of Idealab, who shared it in a Medium article.

If you've ever found yourself stuck in a cycle of excuses, self-doubt, or inconsistency, you're not alone. We've all had moments where we let ourselves off the hook or blamed circumstances we couldn't control. Real growth begins the moment we take ownership, not of everything but of what's already within our control.

This list, "10 Things That Require Zero Talent," is a powerful reminder that excellence isn't reserved for the gifted. It's built by those who choose to show up with integrity, day after day, in small but powerful ways.

These ten traits don't depend on your background, your résumé, or your natural ability. They're choices, habits, and mindsets that you can start working on today.

Use this list not as a mirror to judge yourself but as a starting point to grow. Choose one or two that resonate most right now, and commit to practicing them this week. Small actions, done with consistency, lead to big transformation.

You don't need to be perfect. You just need to be willing.

Let's begin.

1. **Being on time**—This shows respect, discipline, and dependability.
2. **Work ethic**—Consistent effort always sets you apart.
3. **Effort**—No one can control your talent, but *you* control your effort every single day.
4. **Body language**—Confidence, presence, and engagement speak louder than words.
5. **Energy**—Bring a positive presence into every room.
6. **Attitude**—Choose optimism, resilience, and humility, no matter the circumstances.
7. **Passion**—Let your enthusiasm for the mission fuel your work.
8. **Being coachable**—Stay open to feedback and hungry to grow.
9. **Doing extra**—Go beyond what's asked—not for praise but for pride.
10. **Being prepared**—Read, review, and think ahead.[69]

The best part? None of these traits depend on talent, luck, or a perfect past. They're choices, accessible to anyone, anytime. With repeated, intentional effort, they take root and shape a life of impact. Begin, practice daily, and watch how even the smallest consistent actions ripple into extraordinary results.

Continue Your Journey

Whether you're just beginning or deep into your personal growth journey, we've created resources to help you stay aligned, inspired, and on track.

Navigating Leaders
Awaken your vision. Live boldly.

We believe true leadership begins within as clarity replaces confusion, purpose overcomes striving, and transformation takes root. Through The Results Tree framework, coaching, and *The Navigating Leaders Podcast*, we equip you to live and lead with courage, conviction, and wholeness. Learn more at navigatingleaders.com.

Listen to *The Navigating Leaders Podcast*

Join Gabriel and inspiring guests on *The Navigating Leaders Podcast*, where leadership, faith, and purpose collide. Subscribe on your favorite podcast platform, and get real conversations, practical insights, and encouragement to lead with vision and conviction. Would you like to be a guest and share your transformation? Visit navigatingleaders.com or email podcast@navigatingleaders.com.

Download Tools and Resources

Access free downloads, worksheets, and guided exercises to help you implement the lessons from The Results Tree in your own life. Visit navigatingleaders.com/resources.

Book Gabriel for Speaking

Looking for a dynamic, purpose-driven speaker for your next event? Gabriel Griess brings the insights of a leadership coach, the experience of a combat veteran, and the power of The Results Tree to every audience, delivering practical wisdom, moving stories, and transformational tools. To inquire or book Gabriel, email booking@navigatingleaders.com.

Share Your Story

We'd love to hear how The Results Tree has impacted your life. Whether it's a breakthrough, a transformation, or your personal salvation story, your testimony matters. Email me directly anytime at gabriel@navigatingleaders.com.

Your transformation doesn't end here.
The Navigating Leaders website offers everything you need to keep growing, including the Vision Engine (VSN NGN), free resources, coaching and cohort opportunities, podcast episodes, newsletters, and more. Scan the QR code or visit navigatingleaders.com to stay connected and inspired.

How Salvation Works: A Simple Invitation

God loves you. He made you to know Him and to live with Him forever. And all of us have done wrong things—had thoughts, spoken words, or acted in ways that don't match God's way. The Bible calls this sin, and it creates a gap between us and God. We can't fix that gap by trying harder or doing good things.

Here's the good news: God made a way. He sent His Son, Jesus, to live a perfect life, die on the cross for our sins, and rise again. When we trust Jesus, God forgives. We become part of His family.

The Bible explains it this way:

> For by grace you have been saved through faith. And this is not your own doing; it is the gift of God, not a result of works, so that no one may boast.
> —Ephesians 2:8–9

That means we don't earn salvation. God gives it as a gift. We receive it by faith, by trusting Jesus.

Do you want to begin this new life with God? Yes? You can talk to Him right now. The words aren't magic; what matters is your heart.

A Simple Prayer

God, I know I have sinned. I need Your forgiveness. I believe Jesus died for my sins and rose again. Please come into my life, Jesus, and be my Savior and Lord. Help me follow You. Thank You for loving me unconditionally and making me new. Amen.

If you prayed that prayer and meant it, welcome to God's family! This is the start of a new journey, full of grace, hope, and growth. Tell someone, find a good church, read the Bible, and talk to God every day. You're not alone.

I'd love to hear from you. Email me at gabriel@navigatingleaders.com and share your decision.

Acknowledgments

No journey worth taking is traveled alone. This book would not exist without the steady support, inspiration, and influence of so many incredible people.

To Kristie, my partner in love and life: Your strength, encouragement, and unwavering belief in me are woven into every word of these pages. Thank you for walking beside me in every season and on every stretch of this journey.

To Preston, Mikayla "MG," and Harrison: You are my greatest legacy. Watching you grow fills me with hope, purpose, and endless motivation to become a better man. May you always pursue your vision with boldness, faith, and joy.

To my parents and my sister Rozz: Thank you for your sacrifices, values, and faith. Your protection and love gave me the foundation to grow, stumble, rise, and lead with conviction.

To Keith Bentz: Your coaching, friendship, and inspiration have been with me since the first steps of my transformational journey. Thank you for inviting me into the men's retreat brotherhood and for your devoted support in helping shape the words on these pages. You are loved and valued beyond measure, and the world is better for your lifetime of service.

To Stacy James: Your coaching, accountability, and friendship helped clarify my purpose and gave me the courage to live it. You helped plant the seed for *The Results Tree* long before I knew what it would become.

To Kevin Sellers and my entire team at Excel Medical Staffing and MedForceX: Thank you for trusting the vision and showing me what clear intention and committed action look like in real time. You are living proof that culture and calling can transform lives.

To my Creator: Every good thing flows from You. Thank You for the second chances, the course corrections, the vision, and the grace to keep going. May this book bring You glory and help others step boldly into the life they were created to live.

And finally, to the readers and the brave, committed souls who choose to take themselves on and employ the tools of The Results Tree: Thank you. Thank you for trusting this process, for doing the hard inner work, and for believing that change is possible. Your courage to commit yourself to the path of growth and take responsibility for your vision is what makes transformation real. This book is for you and because of you.

Endnotes

Chapter 1

1 "Thomas Merton (1915–1968): Ladder of Success," The Catholic Storeroom, accessed April 12, 2025, https://www.catholicstoreroom.com/category/quotes/quote-author/thomas-merton-1915-1968/page/2/.
2 "United States Air Force Weapons School," Nellis Air Force Base, accessed April 12, 2025, https://www.nellis.af.mil/About/Fact-Sheets/Display/Article/284156/united-states-air-force-weapons-school/.
3 As I mentioned, I didn't apply to any other colleges, but my mother submitted an application in my name to the University of Nebraska, just a few miles from our home. Good try, Mom, but I had no intention of going anywhere but the Air Force Academy.
4 "God Sees You as Acceptable," Pastor Rick's Daily Hope, accessed June 1, 2025, https://www.pastorrick.com/current-teaching/devotional/god-sees-you-as-acceptable.
5 Simon Sinek, *Start with Why* (Penguin Group, 2009), 39.
6 John Bradshaw, *Healing the Shame That Binds You* (HCI, 2005), https://creativegrowth.com/wp-content/uploads/2017/10/bradshaw_shame-1.pdf, 26.

Chapter 2

7 Mitch Albom, *Tuesdays with Morrie* (Crown, 2002), 43.
8 Eben Harrell, "Neuromarketing: What You Need to Know," *Harvard Business Review*, January 23, 2019, https://hbr.org/2019/01/neuromarketing-what-you-need-to-know.
9 C. S. Lewis, *Mere Christianity* (HarperCollins, 1952), 122.
10 Cited by numerous sources.
11 60 *Minutes*, "Tom Brady on Winning: There's 'Got to Be More Than This,'" YouTube, 2005, https://www.youtube.com/watch?v=-TA4_fVkv3c.
12 60 *Minutes*, November 6, 2005.
13 *Miss Americana*, produced by Morgan Neville, Caitrin Rogers, and Christine O'Malley, January 23, 2020.
14 Brené Brown, *Daring Greatly* (Penguin Books, 2013), 122.
15 Adapted from Tim Keller, "Idolatry: The Sin Beneath All Sins," Redeemer Presbyterian Church, New York.
16 David Foster Wallace, "Plain Old Untrendy Troubles and Emotions," *The Guardian*, September 19, 2008, www.theguardian.com/books/2008/sep/20/fiction. Adapted from David Foster Wallace, "This Is Water," Kenyon College (Ohio) commencement address.
17 David Brooks, "The Power of Altruism," *New York Times*, July 8, 2016, https://www.nytimes.com/2016/07/08/opinion/the-power-of-altruism.html.

18 James M. McPherson, "Citizen Soldiers of the Civil War: Why They Fought," National Park Service, accessed April 12, 2025, https://npshistory.com/series/symposia/rally_high_ground/chap4.htm.

19 "Trench Warfare," The National WWI Museum and Memorial, accessed May 31, 2025, https://www.theworldwar.org/learn/about-wwi/trench-warfare.

20 Paul David Tripp, "6 Types of Grace," Paul Tripp Ministries, accessed April 12, 2025, https://www.paultripp.com/articles/posts/6-types-of-grace.

21 Philip Yancey, *Reaching for the Invisible God* (Zondervan, 2000), 93.

22 Barack Obama, "Super Tuesday Speech," Chicago, February 5, 2008, *Barack Obama Speeches*, https://www.nytimes.com/2008/02/05/us/politics/05text-obama.html.

23 Os Guinness, *The Call* (Thomas Nelson, 2018), 4.

24 Robert Greenleaf, "The Servant as Leader," Greenleaf Center for Servant Leadership, accessed April 12, 2025, https://www.essr.net/~jafundo/mestrado_material_itgjkhnld/IV/Lideran%C3%A7as/The%20Servant%20as%20Leader.pdf, 6.

25 Adapted from Tim Keller, "A Counter-Culture of Grace," sermon, Gospel in Life, January 10, 2010, https://gospelinlife.com/downloads/a-counter-culture-of-grace-6035/.

26 Simon Sinek, *Leaders Eat Last* (Penguin Publishing Group, 2014), xii.

27 Andy Stanley, "Stating Vision Simply," in *North Point Community Church Podcasts*, northpoint.org/podcasts.

Chapter 3

28 *Collins Dictionary*, "goal," accessed October 1, 2025, https://googledictionary.freecollocation.com/meaning?word=goal; *Collins Dictionary*, s.v. "result," accessed October 1, 2025, https://googledictionary.freecollocation.com/meaning?word=result.

29 Stuart R. Strachan Jr., "15 Great Quotes from James K. A. Smith's *You Are What You Love*," *The Pastor's Workshop* (blog), September 7, 2018, https://thepastorsworkshop.com/blog/15-great-quotes-from-james-k-a-smiths-you-are-what-you-love.

30 Simon Sinek, *Start with Why* (Portfolio, 2011), 55.

31 Patti Neighmond, "People Who Feel They Have a Purpose in Life Live Longer," NPR, July 28, 2014, https://www.npr.org/sections/health-shots/2014/07/28/334447274/people-who-feel-they-have-a-purpose-in-life-live-longer.

32 Miguel Ruiz, *The Four Agreements* (Amber-Allen Publishing, 1997).

33 Viktor Frankl, *Man's Search for Meaning* (Beacon Press, 2006), 4.

Chapter 4

34 David Robson, "How Self-Deception Allows People to Lie," *The Standard*, June 9, 2022, https://standard.gm/how-self-deception-allows-people-to-lie0/.

35 Pastor Rick Warren, "It is foolish to buy things you don't need, with money you don't have, to impress people you don't like," Facebook, December 14, 2014, https://www.facebook.com/pastorrickwarren/posts/it-is-foolish-to-buy-things-you-dont-need-with-money-you-dont-have-to-impress-pe/10152912926060903/.

Chapter 5

36 Dan Sullivan and Dr. Benjamin Hardy, 10x Is Easier Than 2x: How World-Class Entrepreneurs Achieve More by Doing Less (Hay House Business, May 9, 2023).
37 Lewis Carroll, Alice's Adventures in Wonderland (i.p., 2021), https://www.alice-in-wonderland.net/wp-content/uploads/alice-in-wonderland.pdf, 30.
38 Malcolm Gladwell, Outliers (Little, Brown and Co., 2008).
39 "3 Reasons People Give Up on Their Goals (and How to Overcome Them)," Momentum Partners, March 5, 2024, https://momentumpartnersgroup.com/3-reasons-people-give-up-on-their-goals-and-how-to-overcome-them/.
40 Nicolas Cole, "7 Reasons People Give Up on Their Goals Too Early," Inc., March 3, 2017, https://www.inc.com/nicolas-cole/7-reasons-people-give-up-on-their-goals-too-early.html.
41 Ty Bennett, "Great Leadership Is Driven by Passion," tybennett.com, accessed April 12, 2025, https://tybennett.com/great-leadership-is-driven-by-passion/#:~:text=Passion%20means%20being%20willing%20to,and%20gets%20the%20job%20done.
42 From MacArthur's address at the Touchdown Club Annual Dinner, New York, December 6, 1951.
43 Edmund Morris, Colonel Roosevelt (Random House, 2010), 46.
44 "Man in the Arena," Theodore Roosevelt Center, accessed April 12, 2025, https://www.theodorerooseveltcenter.org/Learn-About-TR/TR-Encyclopedia/Culture-and-Society/Man-in-the-Arena.aspx.
45 Linda Stone, "What Is Continuous Partial Attention?," lindastone.net, accessed April 12, 2025, https://lindastone.net/faq/.
46 Angela Duckworth, Grit: The Power of Passion and Perseverance (Simon and Schuster, 2016), 8.
47 Kevin Daum, "20 Quotes from Leonardo da Vinci to Inspire You," Inc., May 9, 2016, https://www.inc.com/kevin-daum/20-quotes-from-leonardo-da-vinci-to-inspire-you.html.
48 Chris Hemsworth, Vanity Fair, at "Chris Hemsworth Takes Blame for 'Thor: Love and Thunder' Failure," Reddit, accessed May 30, 2025, https://www.reddit.com/r/marvelstudios/comments/1cgsjhw/chris_hemsworth_takes_blame_for_thor_love_and/.
49 "Chris Hardwick Quotes," Goodreads, accessed April 17, 2025, https://www.goodreads.com/quotes/509819-no-human-ever-became-interesting-by-not-failing-the-more.
50 "Napoleon Hill Quotes," Goodreads, accessed April 17, 2025, https://www.goodreads.com/quotes/235069-most-great-people-have-attained-their-greatest-success-just-one.
51 Lewis B. Smedes, Forgive and Forget (Harper & Row, 1984), 79–80.
52 Lewis B. Smedes, "Forgiveness: The Power to Change the Past," Christianity Today, reprinted December 1, 2002, https://www.christianitytoday.com/2002/12/forgiveness-power-to-change-past-2/.
53 John Rex, "Why True Leaders Never Blame Others (or Circumstances)," Forbes, February 5, 2021, https://www.forbes.com/sites/johnrex/2021/02/05/why-true-leaders-never-blame-others-or-circumstances/.

54 "Jim Collins Quotes," Goodreads, accessed April 17, 2025, https://www.goodreads.com/quotes/8785092-for-in-the-end-it-is-impossible-to-have-a.

55 Dr. Anne Brown (@annebrown2013), "Toxic people create chaos, point fingers, shift blame, and avoid taking responsibility," Instagram, February 25, 2020, https://www.instagram.com/p/B9A5qCj0PjF/.

56 Kelsey Kryger, "105 Toxic People Quotes to Help Get Rid of the Negativity in Your Life," *Parade*, accessed January 22, 2025, https://parade.com/living/toxic-people-quotes.

57 Sam Peltzman, "Marriage May Be a Key to Happiness," Chicago Booth, March 2024, https://www.chicagobooth.edu/review/marriage-may-be-key-happiness.

58 David Brooks, "To Be Happy, Marriage Matters More than Career," *New York Times*, August 17, 2023, https://www.nytimes.com/2023/08/17/opinion/marriage-happiness-career.html.

59 James Kouzes and Barry Posner, *The Leadership Challenge* (Jossey-Bass, 2012), introduction.

60 "The Bison Advantage," National Bison Association, accessed April 15, 2025, https://bisoncentral.com/the-bison-advantage/.

61 Tom Peters, *Thriving on Chaos* (HarperCollins, 1988), 4.

Chapter 7

62 James Clear, *Atomic Habits* (Penguin Random House, 2018), 22, 38.

63 Andrew Lisa, "24 Lottery Winners Who Lost Millions," GOBankingRates, April 8, 2024, https://finance.yahoo.com/news/23-lottery-winners-lost-millions-220024754.html.

64 Pastor Rick Warren, "Testing Comes Before Blessing," Pastor Rick's Daily Hope, accessed April 17, 2025, https://www.lightsource.com/ministry/daily-hope/daily-hope-with-rick-warren/testing-comes-before-blessing-daily-hope-with-rick-warren-september-16-2021-11849846.html.

65 Garth Brooks, "Unanswered Prayers," *Fences*, Capitol Nashville, 1990.

66 Simon Sinek, "Simon Says," Simon Sinek's Optimism Co., accessed April 17, 2025, https://simonsinek.com/quotes/.

67 Vivian Giang, "42 Successful People Share the Best Advice They Ever Received," *State Journal-Register*, February 16, 2014, https://www.sj-r.com/story/news/2014/02/16/42-successful-people-share-best/39008394007/.

68 Craig Groeschel, *It: How Churches and Leaders Can Get It and Keep It* (Zondervan, 2008).

Appendix D

69 Adapted from Zeeshan Zaidi, "10 Things That Require Zero Talent—from Bill Gross," Medium, Jul 21, 2022, https://medium.com/%40ZeeshanZaidi/10-things-that-require-zero-talent-from-bill-gross-cb4f6bf954de.

www.ingramcontent.com/pod-product-compliance
Lightning Source LLC
LaVergne TN
LVHW020434070526
838199LV00032B/631/J